SECRETS OF HAPPY PEOPLE

50 Techniques to Feel Good

Matt Avery

SECRETS OF
HAPPY PEOPLE

50 Techniques to Feel Good

Matt Avery

British Library Cataloguing in Publication Data: a catalogue record for this title is available from the British Library.

Library of Congress Catalog Card Number: on file.

Paperback ISBN 978 1 473 61248 8

eBook ISBN 978 1 444 79390 1

10 9 8 7 6 5 4 3 2

The publisher has used its best endeavours to ensure that any website addresses referred to in this book are correct and active at the time of going to press. However, the publisher and the author have no responsibility for the websites and can make no guarantee that a site will remain live or that the content will remain relevant, decent or appropriate.

The publisher has made every effort to mark as such all words which it believes to be trademarks. The publisher should also like to make it clear that the presence of a word in the book, whether marked or unmarked, in no way affects its legal status as a trademark.

Every reasonable effort has been made by the publisher to trace the copyright holders of material in this book. Any errors or omissions should be notified in writing to the publisher, who will endeavour to rectify the situation for any reprints and future editions.

Typeset by Cenveo Publisher Services.

Printed and bound in Great Britain by CPI Group (UK) Ltd., Croydon, CR0 4YY.

John Murray Learning policy is to use papers that are natural, renewable and recyclable products and made from wood grown in sustainable forests. The logging and manufacturing processes are expected to conform to the environmental regulations of the country of origin.

John Murray Learning
338 Euston Road
London NW1 3BH
www.hodder.co.uk

CONTENTS

This SECRETS book contains a number of special textual features, which have been developed to help you navigate the chapters quickly and easily. Throughout the book, you will find these indicated by the following icons.

 Each chapter contains **quotes** from inspiring figures. These will be useful for helping you understand different viewpoints and why each Secret is useful in a practical context.

 Also included in each chapter are a number of **strategies** that outline techniques for putting this Secret into practice.

 The **putting it all together** box at the end of each chapter provides a summary of each chapter, and a quick way into the core concepts of each Secret.

12
13
(14)
15

You'll also see a **chapter ribbon** down the right-hand side of each right-hand page, to help you mark your progress through the book and to make it easy to refer back to a particular chapter you found useful or inspiring.

INTRODUCTION

Happiness, and the pursuit of making it a permanent state for yourself and those you care about, is one of life's great goals. After all, who wouldn't wish to be completely happy, all of the time? Yet how many people actively make the pursuit of happiness a priority in their lives, rather than simply hoping that the things they do, and the way in which they do them, will make them happy? For many people, happiness, when it does arise, is simply a welcome by-product of events, coincidental and just happened upon, and not something that they have pursued in its own right. Little wonder, then, that so many people say that they feel they are not as happy as they could be, or indeed as happy as they feel they ought to be.

So what can you do to make yourself as happy as possible, as much of the time as possible? One of the main reasons that people fail to maximize their potential for happiness is a lack of awareness about how happy they are, and how happy they could be with a little bit of work. It is extremely easy to allow yourself to drift through life taking each day as it comes, and never taking the time to stop and consider whether you are really, truly happy in each area of your life, all of the time – and how much happier you might be with some careful planning. But if you take the time to really think about your happiness, and where you could improve your chances of experiencing it, you may be surprised at just how many gaps there are, waiting to be filled, how many opportunities to be happy you have, but which you are not currently exploiting. By taking a considered approach to maximizing your happiness, thinking through each area of your life as it is, and as it could be, you will be able to develop techniques that allow you to minimize the effects of any negative influences in your life, and to maximize the potential for positive influences.

You will also need to develop a robust strategy for happiness. This may seem like a strange notion, but it is in fact a self-fulfilling prophecy – by having a blueprint for ways to maximize your happiness you will get the most out of each and every opportunity, and by building a robust platform for everyday happiness, you can maximize the potential for enjoying every aspect of your life. How many opportunities do you find each day to be really happy? One or two? Several? A dozen? The truth is that with the right outlook and approach you can find scores of these occasions every day. But sitting back and waiting for happiness to strike is rather like hoping to win a raffle without buying a ticket! By being proactive in your quest to be happy, and by developing an approach that allows you to spot as many opportunities to do so as possible, you will be able to capitalize on every possibility for improving your life, and to make the most of each and every one, allowing you to create for yourself a life that is packed full of happiness, and the techniques and strategies set out in this book have been designed to facilitate this every step of the way.

Of course, just having a strategy is not enough – you will need to ensure that you find the time and space in your life to implement it, and this can best be achieved by building a framework for your day-to-day life which ensures that maximizing your happiness is a key goal every step of the way, and not something just left to chance. By creating a plan for your happiness, and then rigorously implementing it, you will be giving yourself the best possible chance of making yourself as happy as possible, whenever possible. This proactive approach will exponentially increase not only your chances of being happy, but also the frequency with which it occurs, and the depth to which you can experience it – every day. And the good news is that it doesn't need to take an awful lot of effort to make it happen. By making just a few key changes to your lifestyle, and by adopting an outlook and attitude that fosters positivity in yourself, and those around you, you can quickly and easily begin to implement changes that will deliver lasting happiness. So why content yourself with rolling with life's punches and hoping for the best, when you can take control of this crucial aspect of your life, and make being happy your priority?

But does all this sound like an impossible dream, a Utopian ideal that is never going to work in practice? Well, you may be surprised to learn that in fact the truth is that it is both perfectly attainable, and easier than you might imagine. By developing the right approach to your life, and the various situations in which you find yourself, and learning to maximize the scope for happiness in every opportunity that comes your way, you will be able to experience an enduring and persistent happiness, and also help to create the same for those around you; and how many aspects of your life are more important to your wellbeing than your happiness? And what can be better than making others happy too? (Which, in turn, will help to make you happier still.)

Look at it this way – if you're always happy then it must follow that all the important elements of your life are working well, and that those you care about are happy too. In fact, your happiness will have a direct bearing on the happiness of everyone around you, and in turn whenever they are happy, this will rub off on you. So it is no exaggeration to say that being happy is one of the most important things in life, and if you haven't yet prioritized it, to make it one of the most important things in **your** life, then now is the time to get started.

To give yourself the best possible chance of maximizing your happiness all of the time, you will also need to develop an appropriate mindset, one that not only encourages positivity and eliminates negativity, but one that keeps you ever-alert to seeking out opportunities and experiences to boost your happiness. Learning to take advantage of each and every such opportunity with which you are presented, and learning to find these opportunities – even in the most unlikely of places – is a skill that everyone can master, and soon you will find yourself enjoying a host of otherwise unnoticed, uplifting moments every day. You can even learn to create them from nothing, and to engineer their presence whenever and wherever you need them, creating for yourself a timely boost whenever your happiness begins to flag.

It is worth remembering that just as happiness can occur in the most unlikely of places, and during the least predictable of occasions, it can also present itself in a wide variety of guises, including joy, fulfilment, contentment, satisfaction, pleasure, excitement, peace, love, accomplishment and compassion. These are just some of the ways you can experience happiness, and by learning to remain constantly vigilant for them all, and maximizing every opportunity that each of them presents, you can significantly increase the opportunity to experience happiness in your life.

So does creating a structure for finding and enjoying so much happiness mean that you can avoid ever being unhappy? The truth is that by packing your life as full of happiness as you possibly can, you can restrict the amount of unhappiness you are likely to experience, and you can also limit its impact on your life; however, you will never be able to avoid it altogether. This is because there will always be situations that are beyond your control and which unavoidably impact negatively on your life, but by creating an underlying framework for happiness to carry you through the bad times, you can ensure that their impact is minimized as much as possible, and that your recovery from any setbacks is quick and total. You will also find that you can limit to the short term the negative effects of any unhappiness you experience, so that even if you are faced with something whose impact will endure, such as bereavement or redundancy, its effects will be softened, and will be short-lived whenever they occur.

It is crucial, too, to learn to relax into happiness, so that you avoid having to fight for it – which, of course, is often counter-productive! In today's stressful, fast-paced world of constant communication and never-ending connectivity, relaxing can be harder than ever as it can be difficult to find any real 'down time', moments of peace, tranquillity and calm that allow you to recharge your batteries, and to reflect on just how well your life-structure and techniques for maximizing your happiness are working for you. But thinking that you don't have time to stop and take stock of your situation is the same as saying that you don't have time to be happy. You will need to find ways of slowing down every now and then, and that means taking the decision to stand back from the hectic pace of life that you will inevitably find threatening to take over from time to time – and the means of doing so.

It has been said that you are your life, and your life exists only in each moment as you live it, so making the most of every moment is crucial to leading a happy life, and this can only be achieved when you are sufficiently relaxed to allow it to happen. If you do, however, you will be able to ensure that every day is full of happy moments – and it follows that your whole life will be happy as a result. In the same way that if you look after the pennies, the pounds will look after themselves, so making the most of each individual opportunity you have for happiness, in whatever form, is a recipe for ensuring that your whole life is happy.

Planning for happiness is crucial to achieving it, and part of this means being very clear about what exactly you want to get out of life, and just how much you're willing to put in to get it. Assuming that you know yourself, and know what makes you happy, and that you are clear not only about the things you enjoy (the easy part), but about how you can engineer their continual appearance in your life (the difficult part), you will need to ensure that you create the time and space to make them happen, and also that you avoid the succession of traps that await the unwary and unprepared.

Chasing your tail trying to keep up with other people whose lives you perceive as enviable, or frantically trying to achieve an impossible dream are just a couple of the ways in which the pursuit of happiness, unless it is properly managed, can easily backfire. After all, a robust and concerted effort in all the right areas needs to be matched with a relaxed and unhurried approach, so that you do not find yourself unwittingly trying too hard to be happy, or spending time pointlessly worrying over whether you are happy enough. This may require you to make some significant changes to your lifestyle, but if the result is engineering a way to be as happy as possible, as much of the time as possible, creating a lasting and profound happiness, then it is surely worth the sacrifice. So don't let another moment pass you by without ensuring that you are truly happy – instead, get started right away with implementing the techniques and strategies in this book, to make a positive, and potentially life-changing, difference to the way you live.

Forget about being happy

> *'Happiness is not something ready-made. It comes from your own actions.'* Dalai Lama

> *'Happiness doesn't depend on any external conditions, it is governed by our mental attitude.'* Dale Carnegie

> *'Happiness often sneaks in through a door you didn't know you left open.'* John Barrymore

> *'It is not how much we have, but how much we enjoy, that makes happiness.'* Charles Spurgeon

> *'Some cause happiness wherever they go; others whenever they go.'* Oscar Wilde

A man died and went up to Heaven. He was met at the Pearly Gates by St Peter, who greeted him and asked him how much he had enjoyed his time on Earth.

'It was okay,' said the man, 'but somehow life didn't work out to be quite as good as I had thought it would be.'

'Really?' replied St Peter. 'Why was that? You had a family who loved you, a job you were good at, a nice house, and you were able to take a holiday every year. It seems like the sort of life most people would be perfectly happy with.'

'But that's just it,' retorted the man. 'I wasn't happy. I had all the trappings of success, and I tried hard to be a good person, but none of it made me really happy, and I don't know why. I honestly couldn't have tried any harder.'

'So you always tried hard to be happy?' asked St Peter.

'Always,' replied the man, 'but it never seemed to work. I strived my whole life to be happy, and worked hard at everything I did. I didn't even have time to do some of the things I wanted to do, I was trying so hard.'

'What sort of things?' asked St Peter.

'Oh, just having the time to play with my children more, go for walks on sunny days, try my hand at painting or pottery or model-making. Just silly things really, so I put my energies into the big things, like work, and chairing a variety of worthwhile committees.'

'But that's just the problem,' replied the saint, gently. 'You were so busy trying to accomplish the big things you thought would bring you happiness, that you completely overlooked all the little things that actually would have done. If you had just taken a step back, relaxed, and allowed happiness to find you it would have, but you were always doing so much that happiness could never keep up with you.'

MAXIMIZE YOUR HAPPINESS

Happiness often occurs when and where you least expect it, and just as often it doesn't materialize when and where you had expected it to. So is the answer to forget about being happy? Certainly, allowing happiness to arrive unbidden is a powerful tool in the quest to maximize your happiness, since it allows for it to happen any time and any place, and without any effort on your part. But to simply leave it completely to chance is unlikely to produce the best results. There is a lot you can do to improve your odds of being happy and doing as much as possible maximizes your chances, so developing a strategy that includes as many approaches as possible is the best way forward.

However, doing so in a planned and prepared manner is one thing – spending all your time on it, so you cannibalize the time you could spend being happy, or allowing yourself to get stressed worrying about what you should be doing to improve your happiness, is quite another, and a situation that is clearly counter-productive. Making the most of everything in your life – yourself, your situation, the opportunities that come your way or that you can engineer, and so on – is far more likely to produce the results you want than simply ignoring the situation and allowing yourself to just forget about being happy.

PUT YOURSELF AT THE CENTRE

Draw a 'mental pathfinder' map, plotting all the key areas of your life as it is now, and highlighting those that give you what you need, and are therefore positive, and all those elements that lack what you require or hold you back. Your map should be laid out to show three things: where you are at each moment, what you are doing, and when each event is occurring. Try to put them all on the same map, for ease of reference, and then highlight the positives and negatives in different colours so that you can see at a glance where the areas of greatest strength and weakness are. This will also show you what is causing them, and when and where they are occurring.

This is useful as a tool to allow you to take stock of your situation, and to see where you are currently happy and where you need to improve. Then you need to work out a solution for the latter. Bear in mind that 'happiness' is too broad a term to be meaningful, so you need to understand what it means for you in each situation, e.g. excitement, contentment, peace, fulfilment, etc. Understand exactly what makes you happy, and when it is occurring in your life at the moment, and where else it could be happening with a little careful planning and execution.

STAY TRUE TO YOURSELF

Ask yourself the following questions:

- What do I need to be happy – right now? In the future?
- What does happiness mean to me?
- What in my life makes me happy?
- What matters most to me?
- What gives me energy and creates positivity for me?

- What creates negativity, drains my energy, and makes me unhappy?
- What changes do I need to make in my life in order to maximize my happiness?

It is only by understanding exactly what makes you happy, and how best you can structure your life to maximize the chances of achieving it on a regular basis, that you can build for yourself a platform on which to attract positivity and deter negativity. This is crucial in the pursuit of long-lasting happiness, and it's well worth spending the necessary time to ensure you make it as good as you can. Your needs and preferences may change over time, so be sure to revisit them every now and then. This structure also acts as a useful reminder of what it is that you're trying to achieve, and what you should be doing in order to accomplish it. You will need to have a clear vision of your ultimate goal – what complete happiness means for you, and how it can be achieved – and you need to ensure that it really is achievable, however unlikely. By painting your dream you are much more likely to achieve it, and even if you don't get all the way, you are likely to improve your situation by trying.

Creating your vision, and determining the points along the way, will help to clarify what you really want from life, the things that really matter to you, and this in turn will help you to avoid the trap of trying to emulate others. It is easy, and commonplace, to try to copy the lifestyles of others who seem really happy, in the mistaken assumption that what works for them will work for you. Instead, you need to be true to your own needs and desires, pursuing what you really want from life and creating the time and space to enable it. Since you can't achieve everything all at once, you will need to prioritize, sorting your requirements into an order both of importance and timescale, before methodically working to achieve them. Remember, too, that some things are worth doing, and others simply aren't, no matter how much of a good idea they seem, because they will just take too much time and effort to accomplish – so ditch them and move on.

Putting it all together

Understanding what it is that makes you happy will involve an analysis of your personality, which goes deeper than simply thinking about the things you enjoy. That approach may work in the short term (and even then it is highly probable that you will just skim the surface and miss out on everything else), but for long-term happiness it is important to think through a number of other areas – your values, your aspirations, your altruistic desires, your changing needs, and your vision for the future will all have a significant bearing.

By creating a framework in your life that allows you to cover as many bases as possible you will not only maximize your chances of reaching your goals, but also facilitate a culture that encourages you to find happiness all the time, whenever and wherever you are, and whatever you might be doing. Sometimes, in this way, happiness can come as a complete surprise, occurring suddenly and unexpectedly, and in the most unlikely of places, and it can often be all the better because of it.

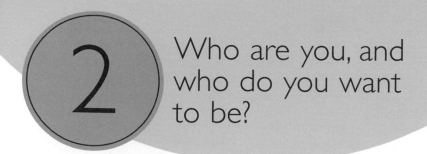

2 Who are you, and who do you want to be?

❝ *'Sometimes I feel like the best role models and the people you should look up to most are the people who make mistakes because they show you how to overcome them and walk through that mistake with integrity and grace.'* Jennifer Love Hewitt

❝ *'Children learn much more from how you act than from what you tell them. There are times this worries me – we parents are rarely the role models we want to be. True for life. True for driving.'* Harlan Coben

❝ *'Typically, when you look for role models, you want someone who has your interests and came from the same background. Well, look how restricting that is. What people should do is take role models à la carte. If there's someone whose character you appreciated, you respect that trait.'* Neil deGrasse Tyson

❝ *"We are certainly influenced by role models, and if we are surrounded by images of beautiful rich people, we will start to think that to be beautiful and rich is very important – just as in the Middle Ages, people were surrounded by images of religious piety.'* Alain de Botton

❝ *'I don't think kids should have role models. They're disastrous.'* Rupert Everett

One day the Pope, the Archbishop of Canterbury, and the Chief Rabbi all went fishing together on a large lake. They packed a picnic hamper to enjoy at lunchtime, and set off to row to the centre of the large expanse of water. There they fished contentedly for several hours, until they began to get hungry and decided it was time to eat. They unpacked the hamper but soon discovered that they had forgotten the wine, and no one really wanted to have to row all the way back to the shore, and then back out again.

'Don't worry,' said the Pope. 'I'll get it.' And with that he stepped out of the boat and walked across the lake to the shore, retrieved the bottle of wine, and walked back to the boat and got in. The Archbishop and the Chief Rabbi exchanged glances, and then they all realized that they had forgotten the corkscrew.

'Leave it to me,' said the Chief Rabbi, and he climbed out onto the water and walked to the shore, picked up the corkscrew, and returned to the boat. He uncorked the wine, before discovering that they had left behind the glasses. The Archbishop took a deep breath, and inspired by the faith the others had shown, he stepped out of the boat and immediately sank beneath the water. The Chief Rabbi turned to the Pope and whispered confidentially,

'Do you think we ought to have told him about the stepping stones?'

The Pope looked back at the Chief Rabbi with a level gaze, and replied: 'What stepping stones?'

Learning from your own mistakes, and indeed successes, is crucial in your bid to either avoid repeating them or else trying to emulate them. If you can learn from other people's mistakes and successes as well though, not only will your pool of available resources widen significantly, but the scope of your experiences will broaden too, and the rate at which you can learn will be accelerated. In this way you will increase your opportunities to avoid stressful mistakes, and enjoy uplifting successes, and by sharing your experiences with others, you can do them a good turn too, giving you a wonderful sense of satisfaction.

Sharing the secrets of your success, and learning other people's secrets and strategies, is a great short cut to happiness.

KNOW YOURSELF

The inspiration provided by role models can be a useful short cut to a quick fix of feeling good. But in order for this to work, you first need to know yourself. At first glance this may sound obvious – indeed, you might well assume that you already know yourself rather well! The truth, however, is that usually we don't know ourselves as well as we think we do. This can be for a number of reasons, which commonly include:

- a lack of self-awareness
- a lack of analytical perception
- not wanting to look at ourselves too closely, either consciously or subconsciously
- assuming that we already know ourselves and therefore don't need to look
- not wanting to face up to our weaknesses.

It is only by really knowing yourself on every level and in every way that you can fully benefit from the example set by role models. Furthermore, getting to know yourself better will also enable you to select the most appropriate people as your role models.

A good way to look at it is to take the example of the training technique that actors employ in order to develop their ability to take on any character. This method, commonly used in drama schools, involves one actor walking around a space in as neutral a manner as possible, while another actor follows them and attempts to copy their physicality, mannerisms and gait. They then swap places so that the one who was being copied can see what they look like. The other actor will exaggerate the points they have noticed, thereby highlighting those characteristics that set the first actor apart. It is only by knowing how they appear to others that they can properly develop a character, since they must first be able to rid themselves of their natural mannerisms so that they always start with a blank canvas.

In the same way, it is only by knowing yourself – your strengths and weaknesses, how you think and how you behave, that you can fully benefit from the example set by your role models.

INSPIRING ROLE MODELS

Once you have identified your strengths and weaknesses, your character traits, how you think and how you behave, etc., you will have a very good understanding of the gaps you need to be able to fill in order to make the best of every situation. You are now in an excellent position to choose your role models, by identifying people who are strong in the areas in which you are weak. It is of course fine to select role models who you perceive to be similar to you, but more successful, or else who are successful in the areas in which you aspire to succeed, but this alone is not enough.

You need to select role models who will inspire you when faced with a difficult problem, by being able to think through what they might do, and how they might overcome the challenges with which you are faced. In this way, you have ready access to a range of virtual advisors, and by following the example you think they would set, you can often surprise yourself by overcoming difficulties that might otherwise have stumped you.

WHO DO YOU WANT TO BE?

Following your role models' careers can be a fun way to share in their successes, but in order to enjoy such successes yourself you will need to decide not only what you want to do with your life, but who you want to be. Try thinking of yourself as the blank canvas actors assume before creating a character. You could be anything, do anything and achieve anything you want to. So what is it that you really want to do? Who would you want to be this time next year, in five years' time, ten years, etc.? What do you want your life to look like? You can think of this in terms of your role models by looking at the life and career of someone who is similar to you, but more successful, and who has achieved what you would ideally like to achieve. Of course, you are unlikely to be exactly like them, or to achieve precisely what they have achieved, but that is no bad thing – after all, you don't want to become a facsimile of someone else, you want to be successful in your own right, since this is the route to a deeper and more lasting happiness.

Putting it all together

Following the lives and careers of role models can provide a useful quick fix of happiness through the inspiration and satisfaction they provide, and it can also give you a short cut to discovering ways of overcoming any difficulties with which you are faced. By thinking through what your role models might do in a certain situation you can often see the problem from a different perspective, and in a clearer light. In order to benefit fully from this approach, however, you need to avoid simply passing the buck, or trying to become someone you are not, but instead develop your potential to be the best 'you' that you can be.

In order to achieve this you will need to be acutely self-analytical and willing to try to strengthen yourself in the areas in which you are weak; this is where selecting the most appropriate role models can prove to be extremely beneficial. By allowing the stories of people you admire and respect to influence your development, you can get the best of both worlds: you can use them to help you decide who you want to be, and to help you to get there. A persistent and lasting happiness is difficult to achieve if you are not happy with who you are, but by improving yourself a little every day you will ensure that you move consistently closer to becoming a 'you' who you want to be, and to achieving the happiness you desire.

3 Investing your time isn't a waste of time

> *'Men talk of killing time, while time quietly kills them.'*
> **Dion Boucicault**

> *'But what minutes! Count them by sensation, and not by calendars, and each moment is a day.'* Benjamin Disraeli

> *'Old Time, in whose banks we deposit our note*
> *Is a miser who always wants guineas for groats;*
> *He keeps all his customers still in arrears*
> *By lending them minutes and charging them years.'*
> Oliver Wendell Holmes, Sr

> *'Time wastes our bodies and our wits, but we waste time, so we are quits.'* Anon

> *'How long a minute is, depends on which side of the bathroom door you're on.'* Zall's Second Law

Following a terrible storm, a group of sailors found themselves shipwrecked, adrift in a small lifeboat in a tumultuous sea. Days went by, until eventually one of the men – the youngest – spotted the lights of another ship. As best they could, they manoeuvred their craft towards the other vessel, and when they felt that they were as close as they were likely to get, they reached for their lantern, the only possible means of attracting the attention of the other crew members. But they had only one match, and the wind was blowing a gale – and they all knew that failure to light the lantern would almost certainly mean that the ship passed them by, and that they would be doomed. It was hastily decided that the youngest of their number should be given the responsibility, since it was he who had spotted the passing vessel and he also had the steadiest hands being the youngest. With a pounding heart, and trying desperately not to snap the match, or allow the flame to sputter and die before the lantern could be lit, he struck it assuredly and quickly put it into the glass housing, and the flame took hold. The lantern soon shone at its brightest, and the duty watchman aboard the ship spotted it, and under the captain's orders the ship came around, and soon the men were rescued.

In life, each moment we live flickers like that lighted match. How will you ensure that your moments burn brightly, and do not simply fade to eternal darkness?

Time spent in the pursuit of happiness is never wasted; yet how much of your time do you spend doing things that actively make you happy? And how much time do you spend doing things that leave you unfulfilled or, worse still, that make you unhappy? To put it another way, if you were to look at a typical week, what proportion of your time would be spent doing things you really enjoy, things that lift your spirits and improve your mood – and what proportion is spent on everything else?

Ensuring that you put aside some time every day to spend doing things whose main, if not only, purpose is to make you happy is crucial in the pursuit of achieving a state of enduring happiness. In the same way, time spent on things that make you unhappy is time wasted – worse, it is time spent bringing you down and worsening your mood, a negative impact that will need to be countered later on. So it is imperative that any time spent in this way is kept to a minimum and that its impact is minimized, while a period of time is set aside every day to enjoy doing something you really love.

A great way of ensuring that you employ your time in the most beneficial way is to get into the habit of thinking of time not as something to be spent, but as something to be invested. In this way you will have a constant reminder not to allow your days to simply drift by, but instead to do something positive with them, and with each part of them. In this way your days, months and years – indeed your entire life – will be filled with things that bring you joy, and your store of good times and positive memories will flourish, further facilitating your ability to achieve enduring happiness.

SPEND TIME POSITIVELY

How much of your time do you set aside each day for doing things that make you happy? Are you consciously opting to spend a portion of every day actively pursuing pleasure – and if so, how much? It is dishearteningly easy to allow time to slip away in a familiar mixture of everyday routines, of doing things that need doing but that may not be pleasurable, and in idling through any down time, so that at the end of a day you find you haven't spent any time doing the things whose number-one purpose is to make you happy. To ensure that this doesn't happen, and that the days without any positive time don't turn into weeks, months or even years, it is crucial to ring-fence a part of your day to devote solely to the pursuit of happiness. By doing this you will ensure that:

- you have some time set aside every day for what you want to do
- you have something to look forward to every day
- you will be able to offset any unavoidable negativity
- you do not allow yourself to drift through your time without positively engaging in those things that make you happy.

Just making the decision to very deliberately ring-fence a portion of your time to employ solely in the pursuit of happiness, whatever that entails for you, is both positive and affirming since you know that every day you will have time to pursue whatever it is that will lift your spirits and bring you joy, time spent positively in the pursuit of happiness.

DON'T ALLOW YOURSELF TO DRIFT

One of the dangers of not choosing to spend a portion of your time deliberately pursuing pleasure is that you may allow yourself to simply drift through the day, unwittingly contenting yourself with offsetting any negativity with periods of time that are just neutral. The short-term effects of this are minimal but long term it can have a significant detrimental impact, since periods of neutrality are in themselves insufficient to properly counter any negativity you may experience (which is, for most people, impossible to avoid all the time).

Taking affirmative action is the best solution and works to best effect when implemented as part of your daily routine, to create a positive lifestyle structure, one that ring-fences pockets of time to spend doing whatever makes you happy, and only that. The moment you stop doing everything else and focus on doing whatever makes you happy you will feel yourself start to relax – the first and vital step. Continued application will result in a sustained increase in happiness, and one that will grow over time. So make sure that you don't allow yourself to drift through your day without ever giving sufficient pause to actively engage in making yourself happy.

MINIMIZE NEGATIVITY

By definition, any periods of negativity in your life will be blocking your ability to be happy, so these must be minimized, and eradicated wherever possible. This can be harder than it sounds since you will first of all need to be aware of negativity creeping into your day, and then have at your disposal the tools to counter it. In addition, it can at times seem as if it is impossible to do anything about it: perhaps you hate your job but can't easily get another; or you are in a relationship that is getting you down but leaving isn't the answer; or maybe you're just too busy to allow yourself time to be happy? Whatever the reasons, it is important to remember this simple three-step process:

1. Clearly identify what is causing the negativity and whether it can be avoided.
2. If it can, make avoiding it your top priority – you will not be completely able to be happy until you do.
3. If it can't, then you need to work to minimize its impact by keeping it as short as possible, and by using the exercises in Chapter 29 – then move on.

Remember, the cumulative effect means that the more time you spend being happy, the happier you'll be to an exponential degree. So try to spend as little time as possible accommodating negativity, and as much time as you can actively pursuing happiness.

Putting it all together

Safeguarding time to invest in being happy is crucial to achieving lasting happiness. This protected time allows you to focus on what really matters to you, and to enjoy doing it. Of course, not everything you do in life can be devoted solely to the pursuit of unbridled joy, but some things can, and most other things can be altered or adjusted to provide at least some degree of pleasure; at the very least you should aim to minimize their ability to make you unhappy. Getting this framework right is crucial in facilitating your ability to be as happy as you can be, for the maximum amount of time, every day. If you are not sure where to focus your efforts, try the following exercise: draw a pie chart to represent where you are currently spending your time. Then draw another to demonstrate those things which give you most pleasure. Then see whether the two charts match. If they don't, you might well be devoting most of your time to things that are not best suited to making you happy, and too little of your time to those that are. So take positive steps to redress the balance.

By investing time in positive activities, and by minimizing the impact you allow negativity to have on your life, you will afford yourself the best possible chance of maximizing your ability to be happy – today, and in the future.

4

Plan for happiness – since you might be dead tomorrow

> 'Be happy for this moment. This moment is your life.'
> Omar Khayyám

> 'Take your victories, whatever they may be, cherish them, use them, but don't settle for them.' Mia Hamm

> 'To be idle is a short road to death and to be diligent is a way of life; foolish people are idle, wise people are diligent.' Buddha

> 'What we have done for ourselves alone dies with us; what we have done for others and the world remains and is immortal.'
> Albert Pike

> 'Life is hard. Then you die. Then they throw dirt in your face. Then the worms eat you. Be grateful it happens in that order.'
> David Gerrold

Later, she would think of it as a gift, but on the morning she had a brain haemorrhage that was the furthest thought from her mind. In that instant everything stopped, and she didn't know if she would ever be able to get it back. As the weeks went by, and it became clear that she would make a good recovery, she began to think of it as a wake-up call, a reminder that she was not going to be around forever so she had better start doing the things she really wanted to do – now. She also needed to take stock of her situation, and make some changes to prevent it from happening again.

The first thing she did was to leave her job, one which she had endured for a long time but which was becoming more and more stressful and was slowly killing her anyway. Instead, she decided to try her hand at the one thing she had always wanted to do and became a professional actress. She had long been a keen amateur, and always excelled, but she had never been brave enough to give it a go professionally. So now she did. Whether she succeeded or failed was no longer the most important thing, but rather the very act of trying, of doing what she had always wanted to do but had been too timid to actually make happen, and suddenly she felt as though she was really living her life to the full, at last, a fact that made her profoundly happy.

She also decided to move house. She had been thinking about it for years, and had even got as far as to have estate agents value her current home, and have a few viewings of the sort of property she would like to buy, but she had never got around to taking it any further. Lack of time, lack of courage, simply never making it a priority – she didn't know. All she was sure of was that she would be happier moving out of the city and into the countryside, and so she moved to a small village with beautiful walks on her doorstep, and a bustling community of which she soon became an integral part. She also promised herself that, at last, she would lose the weight she had for such a long time wanted to lose, and so she began a diet and an exercise regime, and soon she could notice the difference and was thrilled with the results.

In all aspects of her life she began taking things on with renewed vigour, and she was doing the things she had always planned to do, but never got around to actually doing, and loving it. In fact, with hindsight, she considered the brain haemorrhage to be one of the best things ever to have happened to her and she had only one regret – that it hadn't happened sooner. Or, better still, that it hadn't taken a brush with death to free her to live her life to the full.

LEARN TO BE HAPPY

Mohandas K. Gandhi once advised people: 'Live each day as if you are going to die tomorrow, learn as if you are going to live forever.' It's a great sentiment, in that it not only solicits the idea of getting as much as you possibly can from every moment, but to continually improve yourself as you do so. Your happiness can largely be attributed to the experiences you have, on your own or with other people, and to the relationships you foster. By living each day to the maximum you can be sure to never allow an opportunity for happiness to pass you by, while squeezing as much as you can out of every experience gives you more from which to learn, allowing you to seize even more opportunities and to get even more out of them, and so on. It is self-perpetuating, so all you need to do is to get the ball rolling and you will quickly begin to reap the rewards, rewards that will then keep on coming.

Learning as if there were no end has an added bonus, too. Since there can be no end to learning as there will always be new things to learn, so there will always be new discoveries to make you happy, and new information will be imparted and new skills adopted, each of which contributes to your arsenal of ways to experience happiness in your life. Making the most of every day ensures that you will make the most of every month and every year, too, and indeed make the most of your life, and this is in itself a direct route to happiness; coupled with continual and never-ending self-improvement, it becomes a very powerful tool in the quest for happiness.

SOUNDS GOOD. SO HOW DOES IT WORK?

Getting the most out of every day sounds like an obvious approach, and one that should be easy to do – but is it? Well, yes and no. Getting the most out of every day can usefully be seen as a direct route to being as happy as you can be every day, so as a guiding principle this should be fairly standard in the pursuit of happiness. Putting it into practice, however, is a lot more difficult. Some days are simply easier to make the most of than others, since you may be involved in a more exciting activity, or undertake something that presents a more obvious opportunity for learning.

Making this principle work to its maximum potential, however, means that you need to make it work every single day. The key is to ensure that although some days can be made to work better than others, you should never let a day go by without getting at least something out of it. Even the smallest success is better than nothing, and it helps to keep a sense of continuity that will better enable you to get the most out of the most promising days, as and when they occur. It also ensures that you are always in the right frame of mind to exploit opportunities when they arise, and in the meantime each little extra piece of fulfilment or learning will nudge you ever closer to complete happiness.

MAKE THE MOST OF THE BEST DAYS

So how can you maximize the best days, as and when they occur? The first thing is that you learn to recognize them for what they are, realizing when they occur and determining to exploit them to the full. They may be infrequent, so it is imperative that you don't allow any to slip through the net unnoticed. Always be on the lookout for the days that can be fashioned to bring you maximum happiness, or an opportunity for fulfilling learning and growth – or preferably both. Then, to get the most out of them, you will need to have in place a strategy that allows you to dive in as deeply as you can, so that you immerse yourself as fully as possible in the experience, while at the same time affording you the space to stand back to see the whole picture, and to make sure that you don't miss out on anything. Finally, you need to follow up the experience, reflecting on it and reviewing it to fix it as firmly as possible in your mind, and to get every last ounce of pleasure from it, and maximizing the learning opportunity it has provided.

Putting it all together

Making the most of every single day, exploiting it as fully as possible in order to get as much pleasure from it as you can, and also learning as much as possible from your experiences, is key to maximizing your happiness. Even the dullest of days will offer you something worth exploring, and seizing these moments as and when they occur, and getting the most out of them, is a great way to keep your happiness topped up, and to keep yourself ready to take full advantage of the best days. These might not occur often, but when they do it is important to take full advantage of them so that you get to turbocharge your happiness, giving yourself a much needed 'fix' of joy, and also to ensure that they provide some great memories to look back on during fallow periods, and some rich and fulfilling learning opportunities, allowing you to maximize your happiness now and in the future.

5 Slow down for the quick route to happy

> 'Slow down and enjoy life. It's not only the scenery you miss by going too fast – you also miss the sense of where you are going and why.' Eddie Cantor

> 'Perfection is attained by slow degrees; it requires the hand of time.' Voltaire

> 'Wisely, and slow. They stumble that run fast.' William Shakespeare

> 'To build may have to be the slow and laborious task of years. To destroy can be the thoughtless act of a single day.' Winston Churchill

> 'Oh! do not attack me with your watch. A watch is always too fast or too slow. I cannot be dictated to by a watch.' Jane Austen

Polly was a workaholic. She had a good job, one she liked and one at which she excelled, and she certainly had no complaints about the salary, and at weekends she enjoyed spending it, shopping. She was outgoing and voracious, and had plenty of friends at work. Beyond this, however, her social life was rather on the thin side, confined as it was to her two cats. She found the time to go to the gym twice a week to make sure that she always stayed in good shape, but other than that she was simply too busy with work to do anything else. Still, she reflected, she was pretty happy with her life, except for the one gaping hole she had never been able to fill. She was 36, and single. Her colleagues thought of her as a confirmed bachelorette, and happy to be so, but the truth was very different.

She craved being in a relationship, and desperately wanted to be able to share her life with someone, but it had simply never happened for her. Then, one day, she got chatting to her personal trainer at the gym. Susan, it transpired, had given up a very well paid job in the City in order to retrain as a fitness instructor. The reason, she explained, was that her old job had simply left her no time to do the things that were most important to her. It was a watershed moment for Polly. She realized in that instant that if she wanted a relationship she would have to make it a priority, and that meant making time for it. She wasn't single because she wanted to be, and neither was she single because she had to be – she was single because she hadn't found time to be anything else. That night she sat down and thought about what was really important to her, and what would make her truly happy, not just in the near future but for the long term.

The next morning, to the surprise of everyone at her work, she handed in her notice. Then, revelling in the new-found freedom this afforded her, she set about joining a number of local clubs and societies, each of which fulfilled a different interest for her. She also joined several dating agencies. Two years later Polly married Mike, and she had never been happier. She had a part-time job, which was relatively low-paid, but she had realized that the loss of income was a small sacrifice to make in order to pursue the lifestyle she really wanted, and that she had never been happier.

PROBLEM? WHAT PROBLEM?

It is all too easy to race through life assuming that your life as you know it is how your life was meant to be. But what if it isn't? Or rather, what if your life as you know it isn't what you want your life to be? If this is the case, then no matter how hard you work at being happy, you will never achieve the same level of happiness as would be possible if you were doing what you really wanted to do. So the first thing to do is to analyse your life, in order to establish whether or not there is a problem.

A great way to do this is to make a pie chart, filling in the sections to represent where you currently spend your time; then make another pie chart, this time filling in the sections to represent all the things that make you happiest. Then compare the two. If there is a significant disparity, then you will need to find a way to rectify the situation in order to give you the best chance of being as happy as possible for the maximum amount of time. If, for instance, your charts have helped you to identify that you are spending most of your time working but that this is not providing you with happiness, whereas time spent with your family does bring you joy but you just don't get to spend enough time with them, then you need to find a way to spend less time at work and more time with your family. Crucially, the chances are that you really can make this happen – although it may not be easy.

Perhaps you can work from home sometimes, or work closer to home so that you spend less time commuting? Or maybe you could work one day fewer per week? This would almost certainly mean less money so you will need to decide where your priorities lie – but it is difficult to think of many things more worthwhile than the pursuit of happiness, in yourself and others.

DON'T SPEND TIME – INVEST IT

Time is a precious commodity, so don't allow it to simply pass you by. Instead, ensure that you invest your time wisely, using it to bring you as much happiness as possible. In order to do this it is imperative that you understand where your time is currently going, and whether you are investing that time in something that will bring you a positive and tangible return, or whether it is time that you are simply spending. Where it is the former, all is well and good; where it is the latter, you will need to investigate why this is so, and to decide on an action plan that will enable you to change it.

If, for instance, a portion of your time is spent pursuing a hobby, then this is time well spent. Equally, some of your time may be spent on something that doesn't bring you as much happiness as it might, but which nevertheless is unavoidable, such as work. Even then, however, it is often possible to engineer things in your favour, even if they can't be changed completely. But perhaps a portion of your time is spent doing something that is avoidable, and that does not make you happy. In other words, some of your time is being wasted. This is time that could be put to good use by investing it wisely, in something that will make you happy, at least in the short term and preferably in the long term too.

INVEST YOUR ENERGY

Time and energy often seem to be lumped together as though they are the same thing, but this is definitely not the case – and nowhere is this more apparent than in the pursuit of happiness. You may, for instance, have to spend a large portion of your time at work, in a job that even if it is satisfying may not necessarily make you happy most of the time, and this may leave you less time than you would like to spend on more positive pursuits, for instance spending time with your family, or undertaking a hobby.

But this doesn't mean that you have to invest your energy in the same way. By devoting most of your resources to the pursuits that bring you the most happiness, even if you can't spend most of your time on them you can still gain the maximum amount of happiness from them. To ensure that you do, it is important to identify which areas of your life you want to invest your energy in, and which you don't. You will then need to work out how this can best be achieved, and ensure that your strategy is robustly implemented. In this way, you can gain for yourself the maximum possible happiness in your life, even when you cannot devote all your time to it.

Putting it all together

By working out what you want from your life, and pursuing it rigorously, and by investing both your time and your energy appropriately to this end, you will maximize your potential for happiness. One way to ensure that your time is not spent unwisely, and that it does not simply pass you by in a dull, grey apathy, without rewarding you for your efforts, is to create 'protected time' in your life. This is time you devote to doing things that inspire and reward you. In the same way you can learn to focus your energy on the things that make you happiest, rather than allowing the lion's share to disappear battling life's drudgery and problems. While no one can expect to be happy all the time, by deciding which things are most important to you, and which things will bring you the most happiness, you can develop a strategy to ring-fence both your time and your energy, ensuring that you invest both wisely.

6 Stop chasing your tail

> 'Realize what you really want. It stops you from chasing butterflies and puts you to work digging gold.' William Moulton Marston

> 'So many people walk around with a meaningless life. They seem half-asleep, even when they're busy doing things they think are important. This is because they're chasing the wrong things.' Morrie Schwartz

> 'People are chasing cash, not happiness. When you chase money, you're going to lose. You're just going to. Even if you get the money, you're not going to be happy.' Gary Vaynerchuk

> 'You can't win if you're chasing the wrong problem.' Paul Wolfowitz

> 'A successful life is one that is lived through understanding and pursuing one's own path, not chasing after the dreams of others.' Chin-Ning Chu

A woman decided to go on holiday, and chose India as the destination in the hope that it might inspire her. For a long time she had been less than happy, working hard to attain all the things she knew she wanted in life, and indeed needed to have in order to be completely satisfied, but somehow never getting there. It wasn't that what she had was bad, but that what she could have was better. She knew it was. She also knew that India was famed for its sense of spirituality, and directly sought out a guru who she was told might be able to help her. She told him what was troubling her, and he listened carefully, then paused in quiet meditation. Then he answered her:

'You are obsessed with what you think your life would be like if you had all these things you describe, instead of enjoying your life as it is. You have become a slave to your dreams, even though you do not know if achieving them would in fact make you any happier than you are now. Rather than living in the present, and enjoying it to the full, you are using your vision of how much better you think your life would be, as a form of defence, so that you don't have to face reality. You are keeping the real world at a distance, by pretending that it is only temporary for you, that at any time your life will change and your prayers will be answered. But if you stop chasing your impossible dreams, and focus on your life as it really is, you will find that you already have everything you need to be completely happy.'

The woman considered this for a moment, and thought how good her life could be if only she could follow the man's advice. 'So what should I do?' she asked. The man smiled. 'That is the easy part,' he said. 'You need only to make the decision that you want to be happy.'

THE IMPOSSIBLE DREAM

Chasing the impossible dream is an easy trap to fall into, and one that most of us are guilty of from time to time – and, for some people, it's a way of life. So what exactly is it? The impossible dream is that of Utopia, of a perfect life with no wrinkles or setbacks, and a lifestyle that is everything we could ever want, all of the time. In other words, it is pure fantasy. Quite simply, striving for perfection is all well and good, but needing to attain it in order to be happy is not. If it motivates you to do well then that's great, provided that you can still enjoy what you have – a life that may be some way short of your ideal. But what would happen if we could stop chasing the impossible dream and instead enjoy what we have. That's not the same as 'settling' for what we have, but rather celebrating what we have.

If we stop beating ourselves up for not having won the lottery, not living the millionaire lifestyle, not having invented the next 'big thing' or having the job of our dreams, or as many children as we had imagined that we would, or… but instead just stop for a minute, stand still and look at what we have, instead of what we don't have, we might find that we are far happier. It is so easy to think of our lives and our lifestyles in negative terms – 'I don't have the car of my dreams; I'm not as wealthy as I would like; I don't take as many holidays as I would like to; I don't have my perfect job; I only have two children', etc. – but what happens if we rephrase it in positive terms? 'I have a lovely car that never lets me down'; 'I have more than I need, and never have to worry where my next meal is coming from'; 'I even have enough to treat myself to something special now and then'; 'I'm lucky enough to be able to take a holiday most years'; 'I have a steady job, and work with people I really like'; 'I have two wonderful children', etc. In this way, you can quickly and easily turn the situation – any situation – to your advantage, and find happiness by enjoying all the many great things you already have, rather than focusing on the few that you don't.

YOUR LIFE IS ALREADY PERFECT

How often have you heard the phrase 'If you're not part of the solution, you're part of the problem'? But what if there is no problem? In that case no solution would be required, which would mean that the existing status quo was perfectly fine. So what really needs to be determined is whether or not there is a problem in the first place. This is not the same as 'Is there any way in which your life could be improved?', since that holds true for most people, and always will, but instead puts the focus on whether there is really a genuine problem that needs to be resolved in order for you to be happy.

In order to find the answer you will need to be clear about the impact it is having on your life, whether it can be diminished or even eradicated by reframing the problem, and whether it is solvable. In this way you will determine whether there is really a problem at all, or whether it is just the way you are looking at it, the size of the problem if there is one, and how to overcome it. If there is a problem, this will give you a head start in putting it right, and if there isn't, then the sooner you find out and move on the better. It is worth remembering that one man's castle is another man's prison, so don't allow what others think of your lifestyle to affect your judgement – and, in the same way, ensure that you do not allow what you perceive others to have and to feel to colour how you perceive your own life.

KNOW WHAT YOU WANT

What constitutes happiness for you? In the quest to maximize your happiness it is vital that you know what it is that makes you happy, and in what way. This may seem obvious, but it really isn't, and because so many people assume that they must intrinsically know the answer they simply don't bother to ask the question. The result is that they march on through life, never as happy as they could be, and without realizing why. Take as an example someone who has a choice to make with their work life/home life balance – they could work twice as hard and make twice as much money, but be able to spend half as much time with their family, or work half as hard and make half as much money but spend twice as much time with their family. If you were in this situation, what would you do? It is a matter of getting the balance right, and to do that you need to examine what your priorities are, what you want from life, and how you are going to measure it.

Another person may strive all their life to earn more and more money, but no matter how fabulously wealthy they become there will always be someone with more money than they have, someone to envy, and aspire to emulate. So they need to be clear as to why earning so much money is important to them, and whether this is really what they want from life. Interestingly, most people tend to measure their life in terms of successes or failures, and their successes and failures in terms of possessions and wealth. This is in spite of the fact that most people rate their relationships with their family and friends as the most important things to them. So in the quest for happiness, knowing what you really want is crucial to achieving it.

Putting it all together

Being clear about what makes you happy, not just in general terms but very specifically, is the first step in being able to achieve it. Yet it is one which is very often overlooked, since people generally tend to assume that they know the answer, or else they never even consider the question. The next step is to realize why it makes you happy, so that you can pursue it in a meaningful way, and to make sure that you don't fall into the trap of chasing the impossible dream. The chances are that your life is already pretty good in a number of ways, and spending as much time focusing on them as you do on the areas of your life that are not as good is a great way to boost your happiness and your self-confidence, and also to put the more problematic areas of your life into perspective. As a useful exercise, try to find the time every day to think of three ways in which your day has been perfect, three ways in which your year will be perfect and three ways in which your life is perfect.

7 Don't try to be happy

" '*I don't know the key to success, but the key to failure is trying to please everybody.*' Bill Cosby

" '*I have learned that success is to be measured not so much by the position that one has reached in life as by the obstacles which he has had to overcome while trying to succeed.*' Booker T. Washington

" '*By trying we can easily endure adversity. Another man's, I mean.*' Mark Twain

" '*When you have got an elephant by the hind legs and he is trying to run away, it's best to let him run.*' Abraham Lincoln

" '*I intend to live forever, or die trying.*' Groucho Marx

Rachel had never had much luck with men. She was bright, and not unattractive, but she was shy and for some reason she had never been able to flirt. She had tried – at work, at the sports club where she played badminton every Tuesday, even at church – but alas, to no avail. Eventually, disappointed and disillusioned, she turned to a matchmaking service for help. She gave them her details and was soon set up on a number of dates with likely candidates, but although she had a nice time with most of them, none led to a lasting romance. In fact, none of them even led to a second date. After a while, she decided it was a waste of money and time, and was ready to throw in the towel but her friends persuaded her to give it another go.

They told her about speed dating, where she would have ten 'dates', each of which would last just eight minutes. At the end of the evening all the candidates were asked to nominate those people they had met whose details they would like, and if any of them matched then they would each receive the other's information. But although Rachel nominated three of the men she had met, evidently none of them asked for her details in return. The organizers encouraged her to attend the next event, which she did, but having no better luck the second time around she decided to call it a day on the dating front. Her friends rallied round, and signed her up to an online dating service, but her luck here proved no better, and at a loss to know what to do next she decided that it simply wasn't meant to be.

One evening after work, too tired to cook and unable to face yet another ready meal for one, she ordered a pizza for delivery. When it arrived she opened the door, and suddenly stopped breathing. There, with her pizza, was the most perfect man she had ever seen. Not conventionally handsome, perhaps, but with large, kind eyes, and a smile that made her melt inside, Darren stood patiently waiting for the money, while Rachel, flustered and embarrassed, dug around in her purse for the exact amount. When he had left, Rachel was embarrassed to realize that she had forgotten to give him a tip, but she had simply been so taken aback upon seeing him there that she hadn't been able to think straight. The following day she couldn't stop thinking about him, and in the evening, as she prepared her dinner and remembered the sight of him on her doorstep the night before, a ring on the doorbell woke her from her reverie. She opened the door, and there was Darren, with another pizza. She was thrilled to see him, but also confused.

'But I haven't ordered a pizza,' she protested.

'It's on the house,' replied Darren. 'It's something we sometimes do for our most valued customers.'

'But I've only ever ordered one pizza from you,' Rachel said.

'I didn't say our most regular customers,' replied Darren with a winning smile, 'I said for our most valued.'

The following night Rachel ordered another pizza, and sure enough it was Darren who delivered it. This time he asked her out on a proper date, and soon they were head over heels in love, embarking on an incredible romance. It was something Rachel thought she would never experience, and a love that she had only found once she had stopped looking for it.

LEARN TO ACCEPT THE IMPERFECT

Needing everything to be perfect in order to make you happy is a quick route to being unhappy most of the time. If you are only ever happy with perfection, then you will severely limit your chances of being happy since perfection, in anything, is difficult to achieve; expecting everything in your life to be perfect, is near impossible. So does this mean that you will have to lower your standards in order to be happy? Happily, it doesn't. Your standards can be set as high as you wish, but what you will need to learn to adjust is where you set your sights. Having high standards is all well and good, but needing everything to be 100 per cent correct can quickly provide a tangible barrier to happiness. Accepting that very little is, in fact, perfect, and setting your sights just a little lower, means that you will achieve your aims much more of the time.

DECIDE WHEN YOU'RE CONTENT TO BE UNHAPPY

It is impossible to be completely happy all of the time, and in the quest to be as happy as possible for as much of the time as possible, it is important to decide where your priorities lie. By deciding which things in your life you need to be as perfect as they can be, and which things you are willing to accept not reaching quite the same level, you will provide yourself with a platform on which to build a robust and workable framework for happiness. Prioritizing in this way allows you to focus your efforts on those elements that are most important to you, and getting them as good as they can be. The other elements of your life, meanwhile, will have to take a back seat, and learning to be comfortable with this is crucial in the quest for happiness. So decide where you will only be happy with getting things as good as they possibly can be, and where you can learn to live with things being just a little less so.

LEARN HOW, AND WHEN, TO RELAX

Learning to relax and switch off is a vital skill to master in the quest for happiness, and it is just as important to learn when to relax and let go as it is to learn how to do so. When things start to get on top of you, stop actively pushing for happiness and embrace contentment. The chances are that it is just a few things that are causing you concern, and that most of your life is in pretty good shape. So always try to look at the big picture, remember how much of your life is working well for you, and relax. Try using deep relaxation, and remember that relaxation only really works when it is complete – so learn to relax completely.

Putting it all together

In order to reach your maximum potential for happiness, and to remain there for as much of the time as possible, it is important to be able to relax, and not to feel that you are never going to be as happy as you can be unless you are trying hard to be happy all the time. Learning to switch off, and release yourself from the struggle now and then, is just as important as striving to make the necessary changes to your life that you have identified as important in the quest for long-term happiness. Try to prioritize, and when things aren't a priority cut yourself a little slack – the world will keep turning even if you don't complete such and such today. Learn how to relax, and when it's beneficial to do so, and make sure that you can be comfortable with at least some aspects of your life remaining imperfect.

8 Celebrating your successes

> **"** 'The more you praise and celebrate your life, the more there is in life to celebrate.' Oprah Winfrey

> **"** 'The purpose of our lives is to be happy.' Dalai Lama

> **"** 'In order to succeed, your desire for success should be greater than your fear of failure.' Bill Cosby

> **"** 'Celebrate what you want to see more of.' Tom Peters

> **"** 'While we are living in the present, we must celebrate life every day, knowing that we are becoming history with every work, every action, every deed.' Mattie Stepanek

American gymnast Bart Conner was active in sports as a child, starting his gymnastics career at the age of ten and progressing quickly to become the youngest member of the United States Olympic team at the 1976 Summer Games in Montreal. He attended the University of Oklahoma and worked with gymnastics coach Paul Ziert, whose critical opinion was that Conner suffered from a relative lack of spinal flexibility, and had limited tumbling skills. Refusing to accept such limitations, Conner's motivation and dedication to the sport, combined with his other physical abilities, helped him to quickly advance and in 1979 he won the parallel bars event at the World Championships with an original move called the 'Conner Spin'. Despite the US boycott of the 1980 Moscow Olympic Games, Conner had been the first to qualify for the gymnastics team.

Then disaster struck.

In December 1983, just eight months before his home Olympics in Los Angeles, Conner tore his left bicep muscle during a routine, aggravating a previous injury. He underwent surgery and intensive physiotherapy, in an attempt to gain fitness. With just one chance left to qualify, and refusing to be beaten, he managed to squeeze into the team. Then, following intense training, helped the US team to earn a gymnastics team gold and in his favoured parallel bars event he scored a 'perfect ten' to win an individual gold medal.

Afterwards, in a television interview, he was asked how he did it. Conner thanked his parents. 'Come on Bart,' said the interviewer, 'everyone thanks their parents when they win a gold medal.' But Conner told him that this was different. He said: 'Every night before bed my parents would ask me what my success was. So I went to bed a success every night of my life. I woke up every morning a success. When I was injured before the Olympics, I knew I was going to make it back because I was a success every day of my life.'

By taking notice of, and celebrating, all your successes, happiness becomes a way of life. Focus on what you are doing well, and you do more things well; celebrate your successes and you'll create more successes. Success breeds happiness, and it becomes ingrained in the culture of people who train themselves to look for it, focus on it and expect it.

WHAT IS THERE WORTH CELEBRATING?

Celebrations are always, by their very nature, causes for happiness, so celebrating whenever, and whatever, you can makes perfect sense in the quest to maximize your happiness. So what do you have in your life that is worth celebrating? If you spend a few minutes thinking about it, and identifying every possibility, you will probably find that the answer is that you have quite a lot worthy of celebration. Furthermore, do not be surprised if you discover that you can find something to celebrate every single day. There is a trick to this though, and that is to broaden your definition of 'celebrate'.

Usually, we think of celebrations as large events, opportunities to stop and toast important achievements, successes and milestones reached. But why should you limit it to that? Even smaller victories can be celebrated, and accomplishments and successes can be found everywhere, if you know where to look. Met a deadline at work? Lost some weight? Walked further than usual today? Finished reading a good book? Almost any achievement can be a cause for celebration, and by celebrating them all you will have a succession of fillips to bring you happiness, and to spur you on to finding even more to celebrate. So try to be as open as possible about what you regard as a success, and remember to celebrate each and every one.

DO SOMETHING WORTH CELEBRATING

The best strategy, although it is not always possible, is to have an event, success or milestone to celebrate each day, and to have another one in the pipeline. Your daily causes for celebration are of course likely to be smaller than the sort of events you might ordinarily have considered to be worthy of celebration, so the one in the pipeline should be of greater magnitude. In this way, you will have at least one success to celebrate every day, and another to which you can look forward. Remember, too, that it is not only your own successes that you can celebrate, but those of other people. If your partner, your children, your work, or even a family pet does something of note then make sure that you celebrate it, and be sure that you celebrate it with them, for some additional happiness, both your own, boosted by their joy, and reflected happiness spilling over from them. You can even celebrate the events and successes of people you don't know personally, but whose lives or careers you take an interest in, such as movie stars, sports figures or members of the Royal Family. The wider you cast your net, the more chances you will have to celebrate, and the happier you will be.

KEEP CELEBRATING TO KEEP HAPPY

Just as success breeds success, so happiness begets happiness. The more of it you have, the more you want, and the more likely you are to get it. Celebrate the things that make you happy, and at the same time remember that even the very act of being happy, however it comes about, is a cause for celebration. If the sun is shining, and that makes you happy, then celebrate it. If you buy a new ream of paper for your printer, and that makes you happy, then celebrate that. Whatever it is, no matter how small or seemingly inconsequential, taking this approach will give you the opportunity for a quick shot of happiness on a daily basis, and having a larger, longer-term goal in mind will also give you something to look forward to, and some wonderful memories to look back on. Try keeping a daily diary of your successes. Do this for a month and you'll see amazing results, and remember to always look for and celebrate your successes, large and small, since the things on which you focus have an uncanny knack of showing up more and more in your life.

Putting it all together

By working hard to identify anything that can and should be celebrated, you will soon discover plenty of opportunities to enjoy the feelgood factor it brings, every day. Limiting your celebrations to only your major milestones and achievements means that you will miss an easy way to bring extra happiness into your life, now and in the future. By celebrating all that is noteworthy now, and by anticipating all that will be noteworthy further down the line, you can create a host of occasions to be looked forward to, enjoyed, and then to be looked back on with pride, creating opportunities for happiness at every turn. It's easy to overlook those things that you could, and should, celebrate, either because you are simply too busy to stop and take notice, or because you wouldn't necessarily have deemed them sufficiently important to celebrate. But choose to acknowledge them and you'll soon discover that life – your life – is full of successes that are worth celebrating.

(9) Get over it

> 'There is only one way to happiness and that is to cease worrying about things which are beyond the power of our will.'
> Epictetus

> 'An act of goodness is of itself an act of happiness. No reward coming after the event can compare with the sweet reward that went with it.' Maurice Maeterlinck

> 'A successful entrepreneur can't be afraid of failures or setbacks. An initial setback can be a great opportunity to take a new and more promising approach to any problem, to come back stronger than ever.' John Roos

> 'Life is a series of experiences, each one of which makes us bigger, even though sometimes it is hard to realize this. For the world was built to develop character, and we must learn that the setbacks and grieves which we endure help us in our marching onward.' Henry Ford

> 'If you so choose, even the unexpected setbacks can bring new and positive possibilities. If you so choose, you can find value and fulfilment in every circumstance.' Ralph Marston

Ian Brennan had a successful furniture-making business. It had taken ten years of effort, but the enterprise was flourishing and he was receiving a steady stream of orders for all manner of bespoke furniture. Then, in the early hours of one cold winter morning, Ian was to receive a call that would change his life forever. It was from the Fire Brigade, asking him to get down to his workshop straightaway. He arrived to find it engulfed in flames, and despite the best efforts of the firefighters it was soon razed to the ground, destroying not only his place of work but all his completed pieces, and even his tools and machinery, which the heat of the fire warped and melted. Even worse was to follow, however, when Ian discovered there was a problem with his insurance cover, and that he wouldn't be receiving a single penny in compensation.

He approached his bank manager in the hope that he would be sympathetic to his plight, and extend his overdraft facility to give him some breathing space, but instead he was simply informed that as he was not now in a position to repay his debt, the bank would repossess his house in seven days. Unable to replace his tools and equipment, let alone pay his bills or find the rent for a new workshop, Ian had no choice but to clear a space among the rubble, borrow some electricity from a friend's adjoining workshop, and start again as best he could. As he looked around the charred remains of his workshop he noticed that a small section of the remains of a wooden roof beam had burnt into the rough shape of a leaping dolphin. Using his penknife, Ian decided to finish what the fire had started, and being pleased with the result, he decided to try the same thing again, this time from scratch. He had a set of carving chisels somewhere in his garage at home, purchased in a job lot of woodworking tools at an auction some years earlier. Very quickly it became apparent that Ian had an amazing talent for wood sculpting, and before long he was receiving commissions for all manner of sculptures and statuary.

Then, in 1989, Ian received the most prestigious of all appointments – that of 'Sculptor to the Most Noble Order of the Garter and Most Honourable Order of the Bath'. He was now being commissioned by the British Royals, and today his woodcarvings and bronzes can be found in Windsor Castle, St Paul's Cathedral and Westminster Abbey. He has also been commissioned by European royalty and other heads of state, and his work can be seen in museums and private art collections all over the world.

BE GRATEFUL FOR SETBACKS

Setbacks, while never enjoyable experiences in their own right, can nevertheless offer some important opportunities, and if appropriately managed can lead to improved happiness. They can, for instance, provide opportunities to revise your plans for happiness and fulfilment in your life, to take stock and to see if you are heading in the right direction, or whether things need to change; and if they do, a setback might provide the impetus to making things happen.

At the very least, a setback should create a hiatus sufficient to get things underway. If you're having problems in any area of your life, a setback can be seen as an opportunity to take a new and inspiring approach to finding a solution and, used correctly, it can create new routes to happiness. Setbacks can also offer new ways to grow, providing the opportunity to try new things, creating the space for new exploration and discovery, as well as building character. It is also in such times that you will find out who your real friends are. This can be a harsh thing to discover, but it does at least give you the opportunity to rid yourself of anyone who is not a positive influence in your life, and to create new friendships with people who are. Whatever the setback, a positive attitude and a robust response will give you an opportunity to come back even stronger than before, and to prove to yourself that you can do so.

STOP WORRYING

Be careful not to pre-empt disaster, and spend your time anxiously fretting about things, since what you are worrying about may well never happen. Certainly, you can envisage any number of potentially disastrous or traumatic situations or events, but the likelihood of each of them actually happening to you is probably quite remote. Spending time worrying about them is therefore futile, and a complete waste of your resources, which could be put to much better use in the pursuit of happiness. That's not to say, of course, that it is not worthwhile planning carefully for the future, and putting in place sufficient insurance to deal with foreseeable setbacks as best you can, but it does mean that spending too much of your time in this way, and particularly on unfruitful worrying, can be damaging to your happiness. So try to worry only where there is a real reason to do so, and then get over the setback quickly and recover strongly.

BECOME A PHOENIX

Recovering quickly from setbacks is important for two reasons. First, the less time you spend dwelling on your misfortune, the less time you spend being unhappy; and second, by moving on quickly you will begin the recovery process that much sooner. So although setbacks are inevitable, the speed at which you recover from them, and the extent to which you put things right, is down to you, and it will have a significant bearing on your happiness. The sooner you begin to put things right, the sooner you are able to see light at the end of the tunnel; and the more positive you feel, the more inclined you become to put in the hard work necessary to recover from your setback and improve your situation as you do so.

Putting it all together

Strange as it may seem, setbacks can be a positive force in your life. They can offer occasions to grow in new and exciting ways, to try new things, and to review your situation and make any necessary changes to improve your happiness. They also provide an unwitting, but useful, opportunity to see who your real friends are, the result of which can be surprising. But it is only worth planning for the most likely setbacks, and responding to other, more unusual situations as they occur. This is because it is otherwise easy to spend a lot of time worrying over things that may never happen; time which could be spent in a happier frame of mind. And if and when a setback does occur, if you get over it quickly, and decide speedily how best to progress and how to turn the situation to your advantage, then you will have converted a problem into something much more positive, and have created for yourself a brand new opportunity for happiness.

10 If you can't beat them – beat them anyway

" 'Happiness can exist only in acceptance.' George Orwell

" 'A creative man is motivated by the desire to achieve, not by the desire to beat others.' Ayn Rand

" 'The first step toward change is awareness. The second step is acceptance.' Nathaniel Branden

" 'Acceptance of what has happened is the first step to overcoming the consequences of any misfortune.' William James

" 'Everybody has many people inside of them; I think we tend to present the one we feel is most appropriate at first, in order to gain acceptance or achieve what we want. It gets really interesting when this technique fails, and other levels are revealed.' Rupert Friend

Mr Goldberg, a prominent businessman renowned for his thrifty nature, died unexpectedly and, despite the cost, his wife decided that it would be fitting to put an obituary in the local newspaper. Following her late husband's example, she was determined to keep the cost to a minimum, and so, upon visiting the newspaper's offices, she requested that they print her husband's obituary with the maximum brevity and conciseness. The young man behind the desk was sympathetic and compassionate, and informed her that they didn't actually write the obituaries themselves. 'You can say exactly what you want,' he told her. 'We just print the obituaries, but we don't write them, so what it says is completely up to you.' Goldberg's wife thought that this sounded like a good arrangement since she could be sure to keep the words to a minimum, and set her mind to crafting what she wanted to say.

After careful thought and deliberation, she settled on the words 'Goldberg dead', wrote them on a piece of paper and handed it to the receptionist. The young man was rather taken aback, never having seen such a brief obituary, but, guessing the reason for it, he informed Mrs Goldberg that even the minimum payment bought her five words, so would she like to rethink what she wanted to say in order to use them all? Mrs Goldberg didn't have to be asked twice, and retired once more to rethink her wording. After further careful thought she again approached the desk, having decided upon the new obituary, of which she felt sure her late husband would have approved. 'Right,' said the young man, reaching for a new piece of paper. 'I'll write it out for you. Now, what would you like to say?' Mrs Goldberg smiled and said, 'Goldberg dead – Volvo for sale'.

ACCEPT THE SITUATION

Happiness, wherever you can find it, is a great gift, and one that is worth seeking out whenever possible. Likewise, avoiding sadness is imperative in the pursuit of joy. But some things that cause unhappiness or negativity simply can't be avoided (such as bereavement), can't be altered (for example, job loss), or can't be rectified quickly or easily (such as substantial debts). Each of these is almost certain to cause unhappiness in one way or another, and often in a variety of ways all at once, and to try to be happy despite them is perhaps unrealistic, at best. So how can you deal with such potentially traumatic and depressing situations so as to leave yourself as little scarred as possible, and able to move on?

The golden rule is that of acceptance. Just as King Canute sat at the water's edge and demonstrated that he was unable to turn back the tide, if you have no ability to alter events then it is futile to try to do so. Worse, it will drain you of your energy, reinforce the negativity of the situation, and prevent you from gaining closure and moving on. Accepting that this is so can be difficult, particularly since it may feel that you are simply conceding defeat where your natural instinct may be to fight, but if there really is nothing you can do then you need to realize this as quickly as possible, accept it and allow yourself to grieve. Only then will you be in a position to move on, but you will be in a position to move on strongly.

MOVING ON

Accepting the situation for what it is, is the first step in enabling you to move on – undoubtedly the most successful strategy for long-term happiness. Once you have allowed yourself a suitable period to get over the initial shock, and to grieve, you must be robust in your strategy for moving on. A positive approach is key, one that focuses on successes in the future, and not one that seeks to make amends for what has happened, or to retaliate, however strong the temptation to do so might be.

So what does 'moving on' actually mean? Well, it doesn't mean 'getting over' something. The loss of a loved one, or even a dream job, may be all but impossible to get over, and trying to do so will simply mean wasting precious time and energy. What it does mean, though, is setting yourself up to be able to carry on from where you were before the setback, and not to allow yourself to lose ground. In particular, it is important not to dwell on the negative events, and to have in place a strategy for blocking negative thoughts whenever they threaten to disturb your happiness. Whether or not you want to forget what has happened, or indeed what may still be happening (for example, paying off debts), or whether it is important to always remember (for instance, a now deceased loved one), it is important that you turn this into a positive move, and that you allow yourself to do so only in ways that benefit you, and which do not create a barrier to your current and future happiness.

HOW TO BE HAPPY DESPITE THE SETBACKS

With a neat twist on the old adage 'If you can't beat them, join them', the late American comedian, writer and actor George Carlin used to say: 'If you can't beat them, arrange to have them beaten.' Despite the setbacks that you may face, in the pursuit of happiness it is important not to give in to them, but to accept them, move on from them, and then work to make yourself even happier than you were before. This may sound like a tall order, and it is – but it is also perfectly possible, and not only will it give you a valuable goal with which to distract yourself, it will also give you the promise of even greater happiness to come. Achieving this level of happiness despite the setbacks will probably mean that you need to work twice as hard at being positive, and that you need to be even more careful with your planning and target setting, but if it means that you can return to happiness sooner, then it becomes time and energy well spent.

Putting it all together

Acceptance, moving on from the setback, and then working hard to get yourself back to where you were originally, before finally striving to reach an even happier state, is hard work and will certainly not happen overnight. But however hard it is, and however long it may take to achieve, it is a goal worth pursuing, especially as your need for happiness will be greater than ever at these times. Try to make sure that you have in place from the outset a firm idea of what you are trying to achieve, and a realistic expectation of just how much you can achieve, and by when. Creating a framework that you can then use to guide you as you progress is a great way to ensure that you keep on track, and that you don't ever lose sight of what it is you are doing, and why – something that can easily happen at such stressful times. Be gentle with yourself and revise the timescale according to your needs, but don't fall into the trap of letting this become a way of simply letting everything slide, and achieving very little. Your happiness will depend in no small measure on your ability to progress by moving on and recreating your happiness, by rebuilding the structures that created it for you before the setback. Having the option to then improve on them allows you to create something good out of a difficult time, and to reap the rewards of doing so at every step.

Get real

" *'Being in control of your life and having realistic expectations about your day-to-day challenges are the keys to stress management, which is perhaps the most important ingredient to living a happy, healthy and rewarding life.'* Marilu Henner

" *'You have to find out what's right for you, so it's trial and error. You are going to be all right if you accept realistic goals for yourself.'* Teri Garr

" *'You must accept that you might fail; then, if you do your best and still don't win, at least you can be satisfied that you've tried. If you don't accept failure as a possibility, you don't set high goals, you don't branch out, you don't try – you don't take the risk.'* Rosalynn Carter

" *'I have to be realistic about what I can and can't do. So whatever I do has to really be worth it. I like to master the things I do.'* Queen Latifah

" *'I have an English literature degree. I wanted to be the next great American novelist from a very early age, but I put it aside for a while, because I got very realistic at one point.'* Daniel Suarez

Two men, unknown to each other, decided that what they really wanted to do with their lives was to own a teashop. This, they decided, was what they needed in order to be really happy. They each set about turning their dream into reality, but in very different ways. One decided that if a job is worth doing then it's worth doing well, and rented a shop space in a prime location. He had the interior professionally designed, and fitted out by a top notch but pricey company. In order to try to recoup his outlay, he priced his goods at the very highest mark he thought was feasible, and bought in only the finest foods. But no one came. Put off by the high prices they stayed away, and after a few months the owner was forced to wind up his business.

The other man, meanwhile, took the opposite approach, and decided to start slowly. He took a stand at the market, and sold his tea and cakes there, with just a couple of fold-away chairs for his customers to use. Sure enough, he had customers now and then, but the mark-up on his goods was so small that he couldn't really generate a worthwhile profit, and although he was doing what he had wanted to do, he was doing it in such a small way that he hadn't really realized his dream at all. By setting his sights so low he could hardly have failed to reach his target, but when he did he couldn't help but wonder what the point of it all was. The other man had quite the opposite experience, for he had set his sights too high and was never able to achieve them. The one thing they had in common was that by setting themselves unrealistic targets for reaching their goals, both had failed to do so and, as a result, neither was happy.

SET REALISTIC OBJECTIVES

In the pursuit of happiness it is vital that you set yourself realistic objectives, since not doing so is a short cut to failure, which of course means unhappiness. Planning to be happier is crucial if you're serious about wanting to achieve it – simply carrying on as you are and hoping to stumble across new ways to be happy is rather like hoping to win the lottery without buying a ticket, but hoping that you might find one discarded somewhere.

By planning to be happy, creating a robust strategy and then taking the relevant steps to make it a reality, you are far, far more likely to succeed. Your plans will be significantly hampered, however, if you do not take the time and trouble to ensure that they are realistic, and that your objectives – what you want to achieve, and the stepping stones you are going to use to get there – are realistic too. Setting your sights too low means that they will be easier to reach, and so your chances of doing so are increased, but at the risk of achieving very little even if you do attain them. Setting your sights too high, on the other hand, means that the results may well be amazing, should you ever attain them, but the likelihood of you doing so is greatly diminished. You risk becoming demoralized, whichever of these two routes you choose to take. With the former, although you may be reaching your goals you will see very little in the way of progress; with the latter, you are very unlikely to meet your objectives. Either way, it can be very disappointing. By setting your objectives at a realistic level, though, you will give yourself every chance of succeeding in them, and when you do, the results will be tangible and well worth the effort, making for a very rewarding, fruitful, and happiness-creating result.

TAKE ACCURATE MEASUREMENTS

In the same way as it is important to set your objectives at a realistic level, so it is important that you find a sensible way of measuring them. Monitoring your progress is a necessary part of the equation, partly because it allows you to keep track of what you have achieved, and the pace of your progress, and partly because it acts as an excellent motivational tool, a reminder of just how far you've come, and what your life was like before you started. Just as with setting realistic objectives, though, if your measurement of how far you've come is not accurate then its value is greatly diminished, which means that you risk undermining the entire process. If becoming happier is important to you, then so should be finding an accurate way to ensure that it's happening, and at an appropriate speed.

REALISTIC HAPPINESS

By keeping your expectations realistic about exactly what you can hope to achieve, and by when, you will be giving yourself the best possible chance of achieving them. And by putting in place an accurate way of monitoring the situation and measuring your progress, you will be best placed to ensure that you keep on track with your plans to improve your level of happiness.

The objectives you set must be tangible as well as realistic, so that you can measure them properly, and they should be reviewed regularly, and frequently. Whenever you see that there is a problem, act quickly to resolve it, and again, at this point, be sure to set revised objectives and be clear about ensuring that they, and your method of measuring them, are realistic.

Putting it all together

Your happiness is of prime importance in your life, and achieving a high level of happiness – of contentment, of joy, of pride, and so on – is one of the best things you can do to improve the quality of your life. In order to do so, you will need to set yourself objectives to achieve. These are the basis of your structure to becoming happier, and comprise a number of small 'action points' that form the necessary stepping-stones to help you to achieve your goal, by breaking up each task into manageable sections. Crucially, these need to be set at the right level if they are to be of any use to you. Setting unrealistic objectives, either too high or too low, is a great way of setting yourself up to fail. Setting sensible objectives, on the other hand, and then achieving them, provides a fantastic boost to your happiness, in addition to the benefits gained from whatever it is that the objective in question will give you. In the same way, the system you use to measure your progress must be realistic and accurate, so that you can always be sure of knowing exactly what you have and haven't achieved, and that there won't be any nasty surprises waiting for you.

12 Optimism versus pessimism – versus realism

❝ *'Optimism is the faith that leads to achievement. Nothing can be done without hope and confidence.'* Helen Keller

❝ *'My friends, love is better than anger. Hope is better than fear. Optimism is better than despair. So let us be loving, hopeful and optimistic. And we'll change the world.'* Jack Layton

❝ *'My optimism wears heavy boots and is loud.'* Henry Rollins

❝ *'Pessimism leads to weakness, optimism to power.'* William James

❝ *'The basis of optimism is sheer terror.'* Oscar Wilde

There once lived three brothers, one of whom was an eternal optimist, one a persistent pessimist, and the third considered himself a realist. For the first brother, every eventuality was coloured by his rose-tinted spectacles, and no matter what occurred he refused to allow himself to become downhearted. The second brother viewed everything as a probable disappointment, and a possible calamity, and refused to see the positive in anything. The third brother took a more balanced approach, with a blend of his brothers' outlooks. Curiously, each brother believed his approach to be the best since it made him the happiest.

'I don't know how you can get out of bed in the morning, since you never look forward to anything,' the first brother told the second. 'I anticipate every day with hope, so I am naturally happier than you are.'

'It's easy,' replied his brother, 'I don't have high expectations for things so I am never disappointed, as you are whenever things don't turn out the way you hoped they would. You frequently feel let down, and sad, whereas I expect things to be bad and anything that isn't is a bonus. So I am certainly happier than you are.'

The third brother, overhearing their conversation, disagreed with them both.

'You both have false expectations, and are therefore likely always to be wrong footed. I have a realistic approach to life, so I am best placed to navigate life's waters, wherever they may take me, and while I am ever-vigilant to potential setbacks and disappointments so that I can prepare for them, I am always optimistic about the future, and filled with hope for what it will bring. So I think I must be happier than you both.'

It was impossible for the other two brothers to argue with this, and as they sat quietly in reflective contemplation it slowly dawned on them that they were twins, and had no third brother; yet they had each heard him, and believed him to be right. Suddenly, they heard him one last time:

'Oh, I do indeed exist,' he said, 'but not as your brother – as yourselves. I am what happens when you combine your outlooks.'

And from that day forward they did, and each was the happiest he had ever been.

MINIMIZE PESSIMISM – AND OPTIMISM

If you allow your outlook to swing too far from one side to the other it can damage your ability to be happy – regardless of which way you have allowed the pendulum to swing. As with the two brothers, occupying an extreme is detrimental to your ability to achieve and maintain genuine happiness, since it will leave you unable to focus on the positives, and be unprepared to deal with the negatives. It is the happy medium that indeed offers the greatest possibility for happiness in your life, always dealing positively with events and nurturing hope for the future, while at the same time keeping a weather eye open for any potential trouble, and dealing with it quickly to minimize its impact on your life, and on your happiness.

By taking a realistic approach to whatever comes your way you will be best placed to circumvent any negativity, freeing you to concentrate on the positive opportunities that are presented. Blinkering yourself from the reality of any situation is not helpful, since problems do not magically disappear just because we want them to, or because we refuse to acknowledge them! Equally, by devoting too much of our time and resources to identifying negativity denies us the opportunity to maximize the potential for positivity, as well as laying ourselves open to the danger of seeing negativity even where it doesn't exist – or worse still, of creating it.

KEEP THE PENDULUM CENTRED

It is important to maintain a balanced outlook and approach, but there are two distinct ways of achieving this – and while they both work, one is markedly better than the other at allowing you to be as happy as you can be, for as much of the time as possible. Let's take a look at the least favourable approach first. This involves reacting to situations as and when they arise, noting the level of optimism or pessimism they inspire, and then seeking to redress the balance. This approach, though workable, has two major flaws:

- **Extra work.** Since it is reactive, and not proactive, it means leaving things until the last minute to sort them out, which often involves more work than would oth- erwise have been necessary if they had been identified early, and dealt with promptly.
- **Dealing with extremes.** By allowing the pendulum to swing too far to one side before bringing it back you will be forced to deal with extremes of optimism or pessimism, and often one leads directly to the other as the pendulum gains momentum and swings wildly from one side to the other.

The second, and more favourable approach, is to keep the pendulum consistently centred. If you are careful not to allow it to swing too far in either direction then you will never have to bring it back so far. This approach does, however, require constant monitoring, a proactive outlook, and positive early intervention.

STAND YOUR GROUND

It is easy to fall into the trap of thinking that it is preferable, or indeed necessary, to maintain an optimistic outlook in order to be happy. In fact what is needed is a balanced approach, so that you are always best placed to prepare for setbacks while at the same time ensuring that you are ready to maximize any promising possibilities that may occur, but you will need to try to err on the side of optimism so that your general disposition is one of hope and positive expectation.

Crucial to making this work for you is the ability to maintain a perspective on your position, in order to ensure that you always remain where you need to be. As eventualities occur you will naturally be pulled in one direction or the other, so it is important that you realize this as soon as possible and work to correct it at the earliest possible moment. By standing your ground and remaining centred at all times you will give yourself the best opportunity to take advantage of opportunities to maximize your happiness, and to do so straightaway, while at the same time safeguarding your happiness now, and in the future.

Putting it all together

Your outlook and general approach to life are key governing factors in your overall ability to be happy. By adopting, and maintaining, a realistic outlook just tinged with optimism, you will help to ensure that your demeanour always benefits from hopeful anticipation, while at the same time safeguarding yourself from persistent optimistic expectation. By hoping for the best, while always being prepared for the worst, you will put yourself in the best possible position to maximize any opportunities for happiness, and to minimize those that might negatively impact it. While it may seem strange not to simply adopt an attitude and approach of outright optimism, if you want to be as happy as possible, the truth is that the blinkers of such naive optimism can leave you open to being blindsided by misfortune. It is thus far better to be alert to the possibilities of events or situations that may cause unhappiness, so that you are ready and prepared to deal with them, rather than to bury your head in the sand and pretend that such things are not possible in your life. A realistic outlook, neither overly optimistic nor pessimistic, is therefore the most likely to enable you to maximize your potential for happiness, and to safeguard it when you have it.

13 Stop worrying about being happy

> 'Worry is the interest paid by those who borrow trouble.'
> George Washington

> 'There is nothing that wastes the body like worry'
> Mohandas K. Gandhi

> 'Worry never robs tomorrow of its sorrow, it only saps today of its joy.' Leo Buscaglia

> 'If you look into your own heart, and you find nothing wrong there, what is there to worry about? What is there to fear?' Confucius

> 'The reason why worry kills more people than work is that more people worry than work.' Robert Frost

A man had noticed that his neighbour was perpetually anxious, but had never known the reason why. One day he saw him outside in his garden, which was rare since he seldom left the house, and he asked him what the matter was.

'I could die any day,' said the neighbour, 'so today might be my last. Under such circumstances it is very difficult to be happy.'

'I see,' said the man. 'I'm very sorry. How long have the doctors given you?'

'Oh no, I'm not ill, so far as I know,' replied the neighbour. 'But any of us could die at any moment, couldn't we? Best to be prepared. So I make sure it's always at the front of my mind. That way I won't be taken by surprise.'

'That's true,' the man agreed, 'but on the other hand, by spending your whole life worrying about death you are not really living at all, are you? You know that death is inevitable, one day, and that there is nothing you can do to prevent it, so surely it is better not to dwell on it in the meantime. Instead, you can celebrate all the good things life has given you, and enjoy yourself to the full. No point in borrowing trouble.'

The neighbour knew that what the man said made sense, and that he was right, but he had become so accustomed to worrying that he was unable to stop, and before long, he had worried himself into an early grave.

Although worry and anxiety are both natural and commonplace responses to many situations that arise in our lives, they must be minimized and controlled if we are to be as happy as we can be. Worrying about being happy – why you're not, whether there is anything you can do about it, whether you will be tomorrow – is a self-defeating exercise. All the time you spend worrying is time during which you cannot be happy, and conversely, all the time you spend being happy is time during which you're not worrying. So focusing on ridding your life of worry and anxiety as much as possible, and of minimizing its impact when it does occur, is crucial in the pursuit of sustainable happiness.

Plenty of problems are only problems if you let them become so – if they're not big enough to warrant concern just cut away from them and move on.

FOCUS ON WHAT MAKES YOU MISERABLE

In order to effectively deal with worry and anxiety, it is important to realize what it is that causes them in your life. The chances are that they are not something different every time, (from a vast pool of possible areas of concern), but that the sources of your worry are relatively few, and that they often repeat themselves. Be aware that they can manifest themselves in different ways according to each new situation, which can certainly make it more difficult to spot them, but if you get used to identifying them and working out what the root cause of each is – what it is that underlies each anxiety – you will quickly begin to see a pattern emerging. This is, in itself, a comfort since you will see that you are not being attacked on all sides, but that your 'anxiety stems' are in fact few in number, and if you can work to understand what causes them, and what are the likely reactions you will feel as a result, you will be well on the way to diminishing their effectiveness, if not ridding yourself of them altogether.

As an exercise to help you to achieve this, try keeping an 'Anxiety Diary' in which you record all the instances of worry and anxiety you experience over a period of time. The length of this is up to you, depending on how frequently you worry, and over what period of time you will need to record events in order to establish any patterns that might be present, but try to make it at least a week, and no longer than a month. This way you will build up a clear picture of the anxiety in your life, without overloading yourself with information.

DEAR DIARY

By keeping an Anxiety Diary over a suitable period of time, you will be able to see certain patterns emerging. Things to look out for include:

- Repetitions of the same, or similar, events
- The frequency with which they occur
- How long does the worrying last?
- Are there any peculiarities common to some or all?
- Is there anything that triggers them?
- How do they manifest themselves?
- How strong are the feelings they create?
- What do you do to try to rid yourself of the anxiety?

Now try to group them, not by what they are or how they present themselves, but by what causes them. These are the 'anxiety stems', the root causes behind the worry. Then repeat the exercise you've just done. By identifying what causes you to worry, what triggers it, and how often it occurs, you will be able to develop a strategy to deal with it; and by understanding how exactly it makes you feel, and how you can effectively combat not only those feelings but what causes them, you will be able to manage them, and perhaps even get rid of them.

FIGHT BACK

Most people, when combating worry or anxiety, do so in a reactive manner, fighting the fires as and when they occur. This approach has two significant drawbacks, however:

- Lack of preparation means the response will not be as robust as it should be
- Lack of time to create and implement a response.

By putting yourself in the position of not having enough time either to prepare or to react, you are severely limiting your chances of success. And with something as important as your happiness, why leave anything to chance? It is far better to prepare early, and to give yourself all the time you need to deal with any threats to your happiness by way of worries or anxieties, and thereby maximize your chances of success. By identifying the patterns of your worrying, and by highlighting the root causes and identifying the best ways to deal with them, you will be creating a robust, proactive approach to managing your anxiety. And with that taken care of, there's one less thing to worry about.

Putting it all together

It is perfectly natural to worry, and to experience anxiety; what matters is how you deal with it. And if you permit yourself to worry about whether or not you are happy, you are simply adding an extra, and completely unnecessary, concern. Try instead to devote your time and energy to developing a comprehensive strategy to head off worries at the pass, as early as you can, so that they're gone before they can properly establish themselves. Not having such a strategy will undermine your ability to be happy, but simply knowing that yours is in place, safeguarding your happiness, will give you an excellent reason to be happy. Better still, it is a real and genuine reason, since worries and anxieties can erode the very foundation of your happiness; so having a way to deal with them is vital in your quest to maximize your potential for happiness.

14 Compared to other people, you're rubbish

66 *'Try not to get lost in comparing yourself to others. Discover your gifts and let them shine!'* Jennie Finch

66 *'To thine own self be true,*
And it must follow, as the night the day, thou canst not then be false to any man.' William Shakespeare

66 *'When you are content to be simply yourself and don't compare or compete, everybody will respect you.'* Laozi

66 *'I don't listen to what people say about me and I don't read what they write about me. People can compare me to anyone they want to, but I'm not going to worry about it.'* Eric Davis

66 *'Don't compare yourself with someone else's version of happy or thin. Accepting yourself burns the most calories.'* Caroline Rhea

Three sisters, identical triplets, grew up in a happy and contented environment and wished for nothing, until they reached an age when their looks matured – for they grew into stunningly beautiful young women. One of the three delighted in her looks, and was always keen to compare herself to others who were not so pretty; at first this greatly pleased her, but over time she became vain and unpleasant to be around. Another of the sisters closely studied every other young woman she saw, convinced that one day she would see someone even more beautiful than she was; when she did, she was devastated, and with great envy fixated on the other woman's beauty until she was cynical and filled with hatred towards her. The final sister, determined never to fall into the trap of comparing herself with others, grew up to be confident but not conceited, and by not becoming obsessed with her looks she was always able to see the best in other people, whatever talents they had. Over time, the first two sisters lost their looks as their faces betrayed their feelings and true nature; but the third sister, although she never cared to notice it, grew more beautiful every day.

While it can be very difficult to resist the temptation to compare yourself to other people, it is usually best avoided. As the American writer and poet, Max Ehrmann, wrote in his famous 'Desiderata': 'If you compare yourself with others, you may become vain and bitter; for always there will be greater and lesser persons than yourself.' Which means that you will always be somewhere in the middle, so comparisons of this sort are not only potentially destructive, they are also valueless. Far more profitable, and constructive, is to learn to focus on yourself and finding ways to be the best 'you' you can be – regardless of what everyone else is doing.

COMPARE YOURSELF TO OTHER PEOPLE – THEN DITCH THE COMPARISONS

To understand why comparing yourself to other people is unprofitable, and to see it in action, try it now. Think of the most successful person you know and picture their lifestyle. Then think of the least successful person you know and do likewise. The chances are that you will run through a mental checklist such as: What sort of house do they live in? What type of car do they drive? What job do they have? Where do they go on holiday? How much money do they have? And so on. And the chances are that thinking about the first person depresses you and makes you feel that you are not achieving as much with your life as you would wish, while thinking about the second person makes you feel successful. There are, however, two fundamental flaws with this approach.

First, trying to emulate those with more money than you have is a never-ending quest, since no matter how much you have there will always be someone with more. Buy a large house with a large garden and you'll be envious of the neighbour with a swimming pool. Build a swimming pool and you'll envy those with stables. Build stables and you'll begin to notice those with a Ferrari/helicopter/foreign holiday homes, and so on. The point is, where does it end? And the answer, quite simply, is that it doesn't.

Second, the only focus of this line of thinking is material, and it doesn't take into account what you want to achieve, or what would actually make you happy. For many people, owning a modest home but having the time to enjoy it, and the time to spend with their family, is what really matters – not owning a fancy car or a helicopter!

FOCUS ON WHAT REALLY MATTERS TO YOU

It is interesting to note that most people, when presented with the task of picturing the most and least successful people they know, think of those with the most and least money – not those who are the happiest and most contented, regardless of their wealth or lack of it, and those who are least happy, even though they might be millionaires. In the pursuit of happiness it is important to realize what really matters to you, what it is that will make you happy, irrespective of what makes others happy – or at least appears to. So often we just assume that wealthy people must be happy since they can buy anything they want, but of course it doesn't necessarily work this way at all. Equally, a large proportion of lottery winners say they wish they had never won, since their windfall brought with it angst, not happiness. So understanding what you want from life, however modest that might be, and working hard to pursue it, is the best strategy for achieving true, and lasting, happiness.

COMPARE YOURSELF WITH HOW YOU ASPIRE TO BE

Rather than comparing yourself to other people, try comparing yourself, and your situation, with how you would like them to be. Remember to focus on what really matters to you, and forget about what other people may think of your goals – the only person who matters in this equation is you. It is very easy to get caught up in the rat race of feeling that you must always have more of everything, and that if you ever reach a point at which you are content with what you have then you lack ambition and are therefore in some way a failure, because you have stopped striving to better your position.

But hang on a minute – if you are genuinely content, and therefore happy, what does it matter? More importantly, if you have reached this state in your life then you should be proud of your achievement, and you should celebrate it – it is, after all, what we are all striving to achieve. So forget about trying to 'keep up with the Joneses' and take stock of your situation, and visualize how you would like it to be – then put in place a plan to make it a reality.

Putting it all together

Comparing yourself to other people, and comparing their situation and lifestyle to your own, is rarely profitable, and can in fact be detrimental to your happiness. What matters is whether you are happy, not how you get there or what trappings you acquire along the way, so try to focus on what you need to achieve this. Analyse your situation and determine which parts of your life are making you happy and which are not, then work to accentuate the former and eradicate the latter. Often this means changing a facet of your lifestyle, and while there are quick wins to be had it is true that in many cases it is a long-term change that is needed – and these can take a longer time to implement. Provided that you are clear on their purpose, however, and that you believe that they really will work, it will be well worth investing the time and effort to see them through and effect the changes you have identified.

Remember that focusing on yourself, and what you need, is not selfish – it may well involve other people, and very likely in a way that will make them happier too – but rather it is necessary, since without it your focus will become unclear, and your goals will lack clarity and become difficult to implement. It will also make it harder to track the changes to ensure that they really are working for you, which is, of course, crucial; so make sure that you do this periodically and tweak your strategy as necessary as you go along.

15 It's better to be worse off

> **"** 'I have no money, no resources, no hopes. I am the happiest man alive.' Henry Miller

> **"** 'Nothing is more dangerous to men than a sudden change of fortune.' Quintilian

> **"** 'There are people who have money and people who are rich.' Coco Chanel

> **"** 'A business that makes nothing but money is a poor business.' Henry Ford

> **"** 'The man whose only pleasure in life is making money, weighs less on the moral scale than an angleworm.' Josh Billings

During a fact-finding visit to Africa a government minister saw a farmer sitting beneath a tree on his farm, enjoying the peace and quiet. The minister asked him why he wasn't out in the fields working. 'And why would I want to do that?' asked the farmer. 'So that you can grow more crops, of course,' replied the minister, 'and to make more money!' 'And why would I want to do that?' queried the farmer. 'Well, so that you can employ people to do the work for you,' the minister replied. 'And why would I want to do that?' asked the farmer. 'Isn't it obvious?' retorted the minister. 'That way you don't have to spend all day toiling in the fields and you can relax and enjoy the peace and quiet,' said the minister. The farmer just smiled and gestured around him. 'But that's exactly what I am doing,' he replied.

It is easy, and commonplace, to work hard in the pursuit of something that you hope will bring you happiness, without ever stopping to take stock of whether what you are doing is likely to result in what you are trying to achieve, and if so, whether it is a prudent and efficient means of doing so. If you simply spend your time running hard, head down, trying to reach your destination without ever looking up to see what's around you, how do you know you're not already there? And if you don't take time out to evaluate your situation it is easy to forget what it is you're trying to achieve anyway. When the route you have chosen ceases to become the method and starts to become the goal, you know it's time to stop and rethink what you're doing. Often there are long, complicated, difficult routes to a chosen goal, and there are quick easy routes, or short cuts. The trick is to always keep an eye out for them and learn how to recognize them when they present themselves; and always focus on what it is you really want, not what you feel you ought to want.

KNOW EXACTLY WHAT YOU WANT BEFORE YOU TRY TO WORK OUT HOW TO GET IT

When asked what would make them really happy, many people cite money as the answer. It's not difficult to understand why, but a closer inspection of each person's situation may well reveal something quite different as the answer to their prayers. The real question then becomes: 'What will having lots of money mean for you?' Some people believe it will allow them to live worry-free; for others, it would mean quitting their job and spending more time relaxing and enjoying their hobbies; for some people the dream is that it would allow them to be generous to those they love, and so on. But accumulating financial wealth isn't the only route to achieving these aims – and in many cases it's not even the best route. It is also one of the most difficult to accomplish.

Having lots of money may make some worries disappear, such as how to pay the bills, but it may well produce others, such as whether your friends are only there for you because you're wealthy, or whether you should be giving away some of your money, and if so, how much. Quitting your job may sound idyllic but the reality for many people is that it simply replaces hard work with boredom. And being generous is wonderful but it is often difficult to do and fraught with complications – and there may be better ways of being generous than by giving away money, such as being generous with your time, or your affection. So if you know that the thing that will make you happiest of all is lots of money, then your goal is to work out how to get it. But if it is just a means to an end, then you are better off focusing on that end goal, and working out from scratch how to achieve it.

YOUR END POINT MAY NOT BE AS YOU HAD IMAGINED, SO ALWAYS REMAIN FLEXIBLE

It is important to know exactly what you want to achieve, but remaining flexible in your approach as to how to accomplish it is a quick and easy way to increase your chances of success. You may, for example, find the happiness you are looking for presents itself unexpectedly along the route to your goal, in which case you will need to consider whether or not it is worth continuing with whatever it is you are doing to make yourself happy, or whether it is better to stop where you are. After all, if you have achieved your goal then there is little point in continuing to try to achieve it, simply because it didn't happen how, or when, you had expected.

By having a clear idea of where you would like to be, but allowing yourself the freedom to not become fixed on the route to getting there, and by being open to the possibility that it may happen earlier than you had anticipated, you will increase your chances of spotting the opportunities for achieving what you desire as and when they occur, even if it is when you least expect them. So it is important to avoid becoming preoccupied with your chosen method or route for achieving your goal, since it may come about anyway by happy coincidence, but always be clear as to what it is you want to achieve, however this may happen.

THE HAPPINESS YOU DESIRE MAY NOT PRESENT ITSELF IN THE WAY YOU HAD ANTICIPATED

Since happiness can come in many forms, such as joy, fulfilment, contentment, euphoria, etc. it can sometimes be difficult to see when you have accomplished your goal of being happy! If that sounds odd, then look at it this way – if you had imagined that to be really happy you would need to be retired, with an excellent pension, so that you have both the time and money to do the things you enjoy, then it can come as a surprise to find that if you simply reorganize your working week, go part-time and prioritize your hobbies, you are already nearly there! The reason for this is that you had anticipated needing time and wealth in order to be happy, when what you actually needed was time and the ability to reallocate your resources. Furthermore, you may have expected that you would need to retire in order to free up your time when in fact cutting down on your working hours, or working from home part of the week, etc. can accomplish the same thing.

Crucially, if you are willing to encompass happiness in whatever form it may present itself, and even to enjoy it in different forms according to the occasion, then you are likely to find it lurking in far more places than you imagined, just waiting to be unearthed and enjoyed. Don't forget that the journey can provide happiness along the way too, so try to get into the habit of enjoying what you have, at each point along the way.

Putting it all together

Happiness can be both subjective and elusive, but it can also be found in the most unlikely places, and on a daily basis. Failure to be happy is often the result of failure to realize when the opportunity for happiness presents itself, or when it is already there. It can also occur when you least expect it to, and it may already be staring you in the face, so it is imperative that you can recognize it for what it is in order to exploit it. Such failure to capitalize on happiness is often the result of expecting it to present itself in one particular form, and at one particular time, usually at the end of a process designed to engineer it. Being open to the possibility that it may instead occur in another way, at a different time, and may even come as a complete surprise, is central to the ability to seize the moment and experience happiness on a regular basis. By not allowing yourself to become fixated on the means to the end, but rather to focus on the end result instead, and by looking past the route to happiness as you have envisaged it so as to see all the opportunities to experience it as and when they might occur, you may well find the opportunities to be happy occur more frequently than you had imagined.

16 Are you certain you want to be positive?

❝ 'Positive anything is better than negative nothing.' Elbert Hubbard

❝ 'In order to carry a positive action we must develop here a positive vision.' Dalai Lama

❝ 'It takes but one positive thought when given a chance to survive and thrive to overpower an entire army of negative thoughts.' Robert H. Schuller

❝ 'Positive thinking will let you do everything better than negative thinking will.' Zig Ziglar

❝ 'Winners make a habit of manufacturing their own positive expectations in advance of the event.' Brian Tracy

After a cataclysmic storm a man was left in a precarious, life-threatening position, clinging to a piece of driftwood, afloat and alone, miles out at sea. To make matters worse, the weather was closing in, threatening to send him quickly to a watery grave, with little chance of rescue. He knew that in such a position, and with no means to help himself, not even a way to let anyone know where he was or in how much danger, he would surely perish, save for one thing – his unshakeable faith. He therefore felt no fear as he prayed to the Lord and asked to be rescued from his plight. A short while later he heard the sound of an aeroplane approaching and, against all the odds, there it was, a rescue plane that could have him out of the water and heading home within minutes. However, when the plane began to circle so as to be able to help him, he called up to the pilot to decline the assistance, explaining that he had such terrific faith in the Lord, and that having called on Him to help, He would surely save him. So away went the plane, and its bemused pilot, leaving the man to his fate.

A short while later the man heard the sound of another loud motor, and incredibly a helicopter appeared from out of the darkening clouds, and began to lower a winch to rescue the man. But again he declined the help, and again he dispatched his would-be rescuers, explaining that the Lord would save him. As the wind gained in strength and the waters grew ever fiercer, a boat sped towards him to pick him out of the water, but again it was turned away. Shortly afterwards, the man drowned. Upon arriving in Heaven, and unable to comprehend what had happened, despite the strength of his faith and having put his trust in the Lord, he asked God why his prayers hadn't been heard, and why He hadn't helped him when called upon, as He had promised He would.

'But my son,' God replied, 'I did hear you, and I did answer your prayers. I sent you a plane, I sent you a helicopter, I sent you a boat... What more were you looking for?'

REMOVE THE BLINKERS

While it's no bad thing to be definite about what you want to do, and what you want to achieve, if you're too set on the way to do it, you risk missing out on opportunities that may present themselves along the way. This is especially true of a more general quest, such as being happy. If your goal is to do a parachute jump then there are only so many ways of accomplishing this, from training through to completion, but if your goal is to be as happy as you can be there is an almost limitless number of ways to make this happen. Many of them will not alone achieve the goal, but will help either by making an incremental improvement to your wellbeing, or by making possible something else that will make you happier. Importantly, there may be opportunities that present themselves which you hadn't even considered. By taking a fixed, blinkered approach, you risk missing out on taking these opportunities, or even noticing that they exist. Conversely, if you adopt a more open and flexible approach you will put yourself in the position of being able to see all the chances for an improvement in your happiness as and when they present themselves, and of seeing the best way to take advantage of them.

Remember that even if the opportunity is only of a minor improvement it's worth taking, since these add up over time, measurably increasing your overall happiness. So try to adopt the most liberal attitude to becoming happier that you can, and train yourself to spot all the opportunities that come along, and to act on them. Even if you have a specific target in mind for improving your happiness, such as getting out more, taking more exercise and enjoying the fresh air and sunshine, if you keep an open mind as to the possibilities for doing this, and the occasions when you can do so, you will very likely find that they crop up far more often than you might expect, and sometimes in the least likely places.

POSITIVE MENTAL ATTITUDE (PMA)

If your mind is set to 'negative' all the time it is very difficult to see the best of everything, and almost impossible to take advantage of the opportunities that occur on a daily basis for becoming happier. Instead, try to keep your outlook as upbeat as you can, not falsely optimistic but always open to any possibilities for becoming happier that might present themselves. By maintaining a PMA – a Positive Mental Attitude, you will not only find that you are better able to take advantage of situations to maximize your potential for happiness, but you will improve your mood just by fixing your attitude to 'positive'.

Try to learn to look for the best in everything, and to see each new situation as a positive opportunity, experience, etc., and you will soon see how many times each day there are chances to lift your spirits and brighten your mood. And if you have a task ahead of you that you are definitely not looking forward to, try using the power of PMA to visualize the task before you begin, and picture yourself enjoying it and reaching a successful conclusion to make the task less daunting and to improve the chances of you actually enjoying it.

MAKE LEMONADE

It is inevitable that not everything you do, all the time, will go according to plan or make you happy. But as someone once said, if life hands you a lemon – make lemonade! In other words, try to turn every setback into a positive, and never simply accept that something went wrong making you unhappy, and that there is nothing that can be done about it. If, for instance, you try to start the car only to find that it won't go, accept that it is frustrating and not what you had hoped for, but at the same time recognize that you have been presented with some unexpected opportunities to make yourself happier. You can now take a walk and get some fresh air and exercise, instead of sitting in a traffic jam, and while the car is in the garage to be fixed you can get them to sort out the radio, which has been bugging you for a while. You know that it will also be returned to you having been washed and valeted, which will save you a job at the weekend, freeing you up to do something you will enjoy instead. So never let a setback set you back – always find a way to turn it to your advantage.

Putting it all together

Positivity is excellent, provided that it is focused and targeted positivity. If your determination on any given point is simply blind faith, then you are laying yourself open to all sorts of difficulties. Provided that you know what you want, however, and you know how you can get it, being positive, confident and assertive is only going to make it all the more likely that you will succeed. Keep your eyes and ears open to any and all possibilities for happiness that come your way, however unlikely the source, and act on them in a timely manner while keeping alive to the possibility that further avenues might open up midstream, or that those you are exploring may change course. And if something goes wrong along the way, don't despair – try to train yourself instead to think of it as an unexpected bonus opportunity. This can take some practice, and of course it might not work in all situations, but by being suitably prepared you will give yourself every chance of maximizing the opportunities for improving your happiness as and when they occur.

17 Motivation and reward

❝ 'Believe in yourself! Have faith in your abilities! Without a humble but reasonable confidence in your own powers you cannot be successful or happy.' Dr Norman Vincent Peale

❝ 'You are never too old to set another goal or to dream a new dream.' C. S. Lewis

❝ 'If you don't design your own life plan, chances are you'll fall into someone else's plan. And guess what they have planned for you? Not much.' Jim Rohn

❝ 'The will to win, the desire to succeed, the urge to reach your full potential… these are the keys that will unlock the door to personal excellence.' Confucius

❝ 'Be miserable. Or motivate yourself. Whatever has to be done, it's always your choice.' Dr Wayne Dyer

A supermarket chain, having launched a new loyalty card for its customers, was keen to offer special rewards in the shape of extra points earned for purchases of certain featured items. The idea was of course sound, and it's one which is familiar to most of us, but in this particular case something went awry. The problem was that the supermarket was so keen to motivate its customers to keep shopping there, and ready with its rewards, that they misjudged the bit in the middle, the bit where they did their sums. Before long shoppers had realized that the value of the points being offered on some items was greater than the purchase price – in other words, customers were inadvertently being paid to take these items from the shops! One wily, and generous, customer set about buying as much of one of these items as he could, making money in the process, and then sat outside the store giving away the food!

So while motivating yourself to achieve things that will make you happier – and rewarding yourself along the way – is a great way to boost your happiness, be sure to do your homework and sums before you start to make sure that the gains outweigh the costs!

KEEP IT REAL

Achieving your goals is a direct route to being happy. No matter what it is you want to achieve, when you do so your spirits are naturally uplifted since you have realized your goal. And when that goal is something that will make you happy, when that was the very point of the goal in the first place, the feelings of happiness you gain through fulfilment are complemented by the feelings of happiness gained through completing your joy-bringing target. So setting goals and attaining them is a powerful way to make yourself happier. In order to give yourself the best possible chance of reaching your goals, you'll need to observe the following guidelines:

- **Set yourself realistic targets.** If you aim too high you are in danger of never reaching your target, which is demoralizing. Equally, if the targets you set are artificially low then the feelings of satisfaction gained through reaching them are diminished, often to the point of making the whole exercise pointless. So always try to think through your goals to ensure that they are set at an appropriate level.
- **Create a definite endpoint.** If you simply hope to achieve something at some point, then there is every chance that you never will! It is vital to decide upon a timescale for reaching your target, in order to prevent yourself from just drifting and never reaching it. Again, be sure that the date you set is realistic.
- **Set yourself milestones to reach along the way.** If the end point of your goal seems a long way off it can be equally demoralizing since it can be difficult to see it as a reality, or it can even seem unattainable, so it is a good idea to set yourself interim goals as waypoints to reaching your ultimate goal. By making the journey

enjoyable, as well as the destination, you are far more likely to stay motivated, and to reach your target.

- **Track your progress.** In order to keep yourself as motivated as possible it's a good idea to track your progress towards your final goal. Knowing how far you've come, and how far you still have to go, is a great way to help you to get there.
- **Add a timeline.** By putting in a timeline, marking which stage of your goal you want to have reached by a specific date, you can quickly and easily see if you are on target to reach your final goal by the date you had intended.

To motivate yourself along the way, reward yourself as you reach each milestone, and always keep in mind what the rewards will be to make completing the task more enjoyable – and make sure that you actually take them so that you have something enjoyable to look back on, to further motivate yourself.

DON'T JUST THINK IT, DO IT

'If to do were as easy as to know what were good to do, chapels had been churches, and poor men's cottages princes' palaces.'

Portia, *The Merchant of Venice*

Lots of great plans come to nothing simply because it is easier to think of what needs doing, rather than actually doing it! If your target is both worthwhile and realistic, then it is surely worth pursuing, and the sooner the better? You know that it is achievable, and that it would be a good thing to achieve since it will make you happier (as will reaching the milestones along the way and enjoying the rewards), so make your plans, then stick to them and make sure you see them through to completion.

START SAVING

It has been said that if you save all your loose change for 12 months, at the end of the year you'll be amazed at how *little* money you have! So if the reward that lies at the end of your goal is to be sufficiently tempting to make it a meaningful target, you may well need to be prepared to save for it, not in token amounts but in quantities large enough to enable you to afford your reward in a reasonable period of time. But that's no bad thing. The very act of saving can in itself be both motivating, as it acts as a constant reminder of the target you need to reach, and bring happiness, since you know that the reward for which you are saving will greatly please you.

Putting it all together

Working towards a goal that you know will make you happier when it is achieved, and rewarding yourself along the way as you reach significant milestones, are both great ways to boost your happiness, the latter in the short term, and the former in the long term. Remember to keep your targets realistic, and to ensure that your goals really are achievable, so that they have every chance of actually happening, and also so that you can measure your progress frequently along the way to give yourself a regular boost.

When you've decided on your goal, or goals, make sure you create a workable plan to ensure that they really do get done. And don't forget to save towards your rewards. The act of putting aside money, for the purpose of rewarding yourself in some meaningful way when the time is right, is a great way to make yourself happy. Expectation of a favourable event is guaranteed to lift the spirits, and keeping it in mind all the time will help you to feel a little bit brighter wherever you are, and whatever you're doing. And when you finally reach your goal, you'll have a stock of great memories to look back on, a wonderful treat to look forward to, and a real sense of achievement and pride – all of which will combine to make you happier.

18 Do it now!

> 'Happiness is not a brilliant climax to years of grim struggle and anxiety. It is a long succession of little decisions simply to be happy in the moment.' J. Donald Walters

> 'A lot of people don't want to make their own decisions. They're too scared. It's much easier to be told what to do.' Marilyn Manson

> 'It is only in our decisions that we are important.' Jean-Paul Sartre

> 'Stay committed to your decisions, but stay flexible in your approach.' Tony Robbins

> 'High achievers spot rich opportunities swiftly, make big decisions quickly and move into action immediately. Follow these principles and you can make your dreams come true.' Robert H. Schuller

A man decided to propose to his girlfriend, and resolved that everything should be perfect for the occasion. He elected to cook her a romantic meal, and afterwards to pop the question. All was going well, and he rehearsed in his head one last time how he was going to ask her, when she was suddenly taken unwell due to a reaction to one of the ingredients he had used in the meal. So he decided to wait for another day. Weeks passed as he sought the perfect opportunity, and then one presented itself in the form of a dinner his work was giving to all staff members at a local hotel – afterwards they would stay over, and he would propose that evening.

Unfortunately, his boss wanted to use the opportunity to discuss some new plans for the business, and by the time he went up to their room his girlfriend was fast asleep. The morning was no good either since he had to be up and out early, so he again decided to wait. Then it occurred to him that rather than propose and then let his girlfriend choose the ring, it might be more romantic if he were to select one. So he visited the jewellers and chose the perfect ring, except that the only ones they had in stock were slightly flawed, and so he decided to return to the shop on a regular basis until they had one that was blemish free. Months passed in this way, until at last the perfect ring arrived, and he bought it immediately and planned another romantic evening at which he could propose. Unfortunately, that night, his girlfriend broke the news to him that she felt their relationship just wasn't going anywhere, and that she had now met someone else. Heartbroken, he was left only with the ring, and his memories, and the thought of what might have been if he hadn't waited so long.

JDI

If something is worth doing – if it's something that will make you happier then it's definitely worth doing – there is nothing to be gained from delaying getting on with it and getting it done.

Avoid procrastination and prevarication!

For one thing, once you have decided what needs to be done, procrastinating and prevaricating will only delay the inevitable. For another, all the time things are left undone, or at least unfinished, they will be nagging at the back of your mind, causing you unnecessary and completely avoidable worry – which undermines the very point of doing them in the first place! And lastly, if the successful completion of the task will make you happier, then all the time it is left incomplete is time wasted, time during which it stands to reason that you are not as happy as you could be, as happy as you would have been if you had just got on with it – and it's time you'll never get back to enjoy more fully next time around. So once you have decided on something that can be done to improve your happiness, JDI – Just Do It – instead of merely thinking about doing it!

It has been rightly said that the road to Hell is paved with good intentions, and that procrastination is the thief of time, so getting on with completing your task as quickly as possible is of paramount importance. This is one of the reasons why it is so important to establish a workable timeframe in which to finish any project, or the implementation of any plan, that you have decided will help to make you happier. Knowing that there are things you could do, but never getting on with actually doing them, or starting them but never completing them, is frustrating and pointless; worse still, it is counter-productive to making you happier – which means it is making you unhappier.

TURN THOUGHTS INTO ACTION

It is not enough to merely turn your thoughts into actions – you need to do so swiftly, clinically and accurately. Any time spent in the decision-making process, before you actually get underway, is time when you cannot be enjoying the rewards of your actions, so discipline yourself to keep this to a minimum. Moreover, time spent agonizing over decisions is rarely time spent in the throes of happiness, your ultimate aim – and in the modern world we are forced to make countless decisions every single week. So learning to make decisions quickly, and sticking to them, reduces any negative impacts of the decision-making process and frees up your time for more positive and productive use. So whatever it is that you decide you need to do in order to become happier, get on and do it as soon as you can, and try to get into the habit of making all your decisions quickly.

PUSH THROUGH YOUR FEAR

'There is no time like the present'

'Carpe Diem' (seize the day)

'Time waits for no man'

'Never put off till tomorrow what you can get done today'

'A stitch in time saves nine'

There is a reason why there are so many adages concerned with getting on with things that need to be done, or why the best time for doing things is right now; simply, that there is nothing to be gained by delays, and everything to be gained for a swift execution of well thought through plans. And when these concern your ability to be happy, and to get the most out of life, you have the very best reason, and therefore the very best motivation, to follow their sage advice. So why would anyone ever hesitate over getting things underway? One of the most common reasons is fear — fear that you don't know exactly what you're doing, fear over the way things might turn out, fear of looking silly if things go wrong — but don't ever let these stop you. While it's natural to be apprehensive about taking the plunge, it's also a vital and empowering part of the process, and you are far more likely to regret not trying than you are of having a go. So go for it!

Putting it all together

Working out what you need to do in your life in order to become happier is a vital part of the process, but it's important never to lose sight of the fact that it is only a part of the process. Plans, projects, dreams and ambitions are great but only if you then act on them. If dreams are all they ever are, then they are useless to you — worse, they are giving you false hope that things will improve because you've worked out what needs to be done, and they will lead to stress because deep down you know that you are dragging your feet. So it's the execution of your plans that really counts. This, after all, is what is going to actually make you happier in the long run.

Remember, too, that it is not enough just to get your plans underway — you need to see them through to a successful conclusion. So once you've worked out what you need to do, or even just the first stage, drop whatever else you're doing and make a start. Often it's the first part that is the hardest, getting things off the launchpad and moving from a great, completed idea, to a barely started and 'lots still to do' project.

So try taking a leaf out of artists' books. They talk of 'killing the white', meaning getting a painting underway. Even if they only put down a very general wash, in nearly the same colour as the paper, just the act of doing so turns the canvas from something generic to something specific, and it makes it theirs. Taking ownership of your projects, and getting them started, is such a crucial step towards your goal, so make sure you 'kill the white' of whatever it is you need to do. And remember that you have an inbuilt advantage too, since your aim is to be happier, and doing this will give you a boost to your happiness.

19 What's the point?

> 'Achievement of your happiness is the only moral purpose of your life, and that happiness, not pain or mindless self-indulgence, is the proof of your moral integrity, since it is the proof and the result of your loyalty to the achievement of your values.' Ayn Rand

> 'Our prime purpose in this life is to help others. And if you can't help them, at least don't hurt them.' Dalai Lama

> 'My life has no purpose, no direction, no aim, no meaning, and yet I'm happy. I can't figure it out. What am I doing right?' Charles M. Schulz

> 'Passionate hatred can give meaning and purpose to an empty life.' Eric Hoffer

> 'Work gives you meaning and purpose and life is empty without it.' Stephen Hawking

Three childhood friends, upon reaching adulthood, set out with very different goals in mind. The first was determined to become wealthy, whatever the cost; the second craved power; and the third was determined to find the meaning of life. Over the years, each was successful in his life, and in his ambitions, and after many years they got together for the first time since they were boys. The first arrived in a very expensive sports car, and was dressed in the latest designer wear. The second arrived in a chauffeur-driven car, and instructed his secretary (who always travelled with him) to hold all his calls while he met his old friends; and the third arrived on an old bicycle. As they became reacquainted, each told the others of his success, and reflected on it himself.

The first had been successful from the outset, and now had all the money he could ever want, except that now that he had so much he couldn't stop, and realized that he would never have so much money that he would be happy to stop earning – and so could never be truly happy. In fact, he couldn't really remember now why he had wanted the money to begin with, and was at a loss as to what to do with it. The second had been an unqualified success from the start, and now owned his own company and had all manner of staff, but the ruthless approach that had made him successful in business had also driven away his friends and cost him his marriage. He had achieved his ambition, but now that he had what he had deemed important, he couldn't think why it was so necessary to him. The third revealed that he had set off on his quest, quickly failed, but was supremely happy. The others were incredulous, but he told them that although he had no clue as to the meaning of life, he had realized that it wasn't important – what was important was that in trying to find it he had realized the true meaning of *his* life – what was important to him, and what, for him, were the meaning and purpose of life. And since he was therefore able to build his life around what really mattered to him, he was truly happy.

BUILD IT UP

In order to be happy it is important to have a deep-rooted belief in what you do, and the way that you live your life. If you don't, then it will be impossible to be fulfilled, and thus impossible to be completely happy. Finding meaning and purpose in your life is fundamental to establishing a reason for doing everything that you do, and life without a reason is not only empty and unfulfilling, it is a waste of time and, worst of all, it can easily seem depressingly pointless. So try to determine what the reasons for life are for you, what it is that you do to validate the meaning and purpose of your existence, and examine each one to see whether or not you are making the most of them. The chances are that you will have not just one such reason, but rather a series of them. These might include:

- your family
- your work
- your hobbies
- your religious beliefs, or other belief system
- your friends
- your ambitions
- charity.

You might also have different ways in which you live your life, or at least try to, such as kindness to strangers, or simply making everyone you meet a little bit happier than they were before their path crossed yours. Whatever your list comprises, write it all out and then prioritize the entries so that you form a hierarchy of what matters most to you. And now look for the gaps. What are those things that you would like to see featured on the list but don't? Or are there some entries on the list that are things you wish you did, more than things you actually do? Since the items on the list, and your ability to deliver them, are of primary importance to your ability to maximize your happiness, then it's worth investing the necessary time and effort to get it as comprehensive as possible. Reviewing your life's priorities in this way will also act as a good motivator to ring the changes in any way that might aid you in your quest for complete happiness, and to take stock of what really matters to you, and what doesn't.

KNOCK IT DOWN

An important part of the process is that your list, properly created, will serve to highlight all the areas of your life that lack meaning and purpose. If, for example, your work isn't on there, but you have a full-time job, then you have unearthed a barrier to your happiness, since it will mean that you spend a large portion of your time and energy doing something that doesn't help to give your life direction, meaning and purpose, and for which you can't really see the point (other than paying the bills). So this is something that definitely needs to change. There is little point in identifying a problem, only to then sit back and allow it to persist. So you need to knock it down. By eradicating the problem, you are starting the process of putting into action the solution, and only by doing this will you be able to reach happiness through it.

This might not need to be a particularly drastic step either. Just because your job isn't giving you what you need doesn't mean that you should automatically quit. Rather, that you should look to find ways to ensure that your job does provide you with meaning and purpose. This might mean that you need to leave, of course, but it might just as easily mean that you only need to find a new role within your company, perhaps get trained up for a new task or take on a more challenging responsibility, and so on. So go easy with the wrecking ball of improvement that seeks to tear down a problem, but look instead to see how else your situation might be improved, and use that only as a last resort. Above all, though, make sure that you really do something about the situation – don't be content with just letting things slide.

CONSIDER NEW DEVELOPMENTS

Creating new avenues in your life that have the necessary purpose and meaning to make you happy is a great way to give your happiness a real shot in the arm, but be warned – this sort of change to your life often requires a fairly major change to your lifestyle, and this is rarely achieved quickly or easily. It is, however, one of the very best ways of turbocharging your facility to be happy, and so it is definitely worth the effort, provided that you are completely sure that any changes you make really will work.

The good thing is that any changes you do make are likely to have a significant impact on your state of happiness, and also be long lasting. These sort of changes are therefore required infrequently, although it is worth revisiting this exercise every few years as good practices have a tendency to lapse if you're not careful, and new opportunities may arise that would otherwise go unnoticed.

Putting it all together

Finding meaning and purpose in your life is key to being happy, and mentally healthy. It is a fundamental need to feel fulfilled, yet one which so often goes unnoticed, or uncared for. Without having this core of belief at the very centre of everything you do it is difficult to fully enjoy most things, whatever they may be, particularly in the long term. It is also true that without these essentials underpinning your day-to-day existence, you are very likely to feel that there is a nagging emptiness, or even pointlessness, to your life. Happily, the situation can usually be remedied, though it is rarely a quick process, and it may be difficult to implement, depending on a number of factors, many of which may be outside of your control. Since it is so important to your overall wellbeing, though, it is worth putting in the required effort to get things right, and while it may be a slow process to implement, you should continue to reap the benefits for a long time afterwards. These changes to your lifestyle, and to your outlook and perception of what you do, how you do it and how it affects other people, should constitute a bedrock on which to build further happiness, having got the central system just right, and will continue to provide lasting happiness as long as they are diligently maintained.

20 Cut it out

> 'Quit thinking that you must halt before the barrier of inner negativity. You need not. You can crash through... whatever we see a negative state, that is where we can destroy it.'
> Vernon Howard

> 'To all the other dreamers out there, don't ever stop or let the world's negativity disenchant you or your spirit. If you surround yourself with love and the right people, anything is possible.'
> Adam Green

> 'The first recipe for happiness is: avoid too lengthy meditation on the past.' André Maurois

> 'That's my gift. I let that negativity roll off me like water off a duck's back. If it's not positive, I didn't hear it. If you can overcome that, fights are easy.' George Foreman

> 'Life is too short to spend in negativity. So I have made a conscious effort to not be where I don't want to be.' Hugh Dillon

Sports professionals are taught the art of positive visualization to help them to achieve their goals – and the first step in that process is the elimination of any negativity. This is important in all disciplines, but nowhere more so than in sprinting, where an entire race can last less than ten seconds, and where even a tiny amount of negativity can mean the difference between winning and losing. It's all but impossible to run as fast as you can if you have a nagging doubt about your ability, so ridding yourself of this mental baggage is crucial. What is especially interesting, though, is that the process sprinters use to accomplish this must be completed before every single race, and in good time — it's no good waiting until you're on the starting line. The same approach should be taken by everyone, no matter what their walk of life. Take some time each day to rid yourself of any negativity in your life, and revel in the freedom and energy of your new-found positivity.

Any form of negativity is a persistent drain on your happiness, and on your ability to be happy. It is especially damaging since it is ever present, often lurking unnoticed in the background, but always there, chipping away at your confidence and undermining your happiness. Even if your negativity stems from just one identifiable area of your life, and only there, its pervasive nature means that it will almost certainly have a much more far-reaching influence, with its negative undercurrents seeping into every aspect of your life. It is difficult to focus exclusively on the joy any situation might afford when you are plagued with a constant nagging doubt or fear, a thorn in your mental side that refuses to leave you alone. It is therefore imperative that you learn to identify any areas of your life into which negativity has been allowed to creep, and that you then work to eradicate it as quickly and as fully as you can.

TIGHTEN THE TAP

Happiness, and your ability to achieve it, can be likened to a water cooler with a tap at the bottom. The container represents your capacity for happiness — fill it to the brim and you will be completely and utterly happy. There are, however, three challenges to achieving this:

- Events that cause you unhappiness, which are the cups collecting some of the water.

- Ensuring you have sufficient fresh or renewable sources of happiness to keep your water cooler topped up, and to replace any water that escapes.

- Keeping the tap at the bottom fully closed. Any long-term situations that are detrimental to your happiness (such as depression) can be seen as the tap being left open. Any smaller scale, but persistent drain on your happiness, is the tap being left to constantly drip. This is the effect of negativity in your life.

Clearly, if the tap is left to drip constantly, then there will be a constant drain on your happiness; and the longer it is left in this state without being remedied, the more water will drip out – meaning that you will need to find more and more ways to keep the container topped up, just to maintain equilibrium. It is far better, then, to work at keeping the tap tightly closed and maintaining it that way, shutting off the drain on your happiness at source.

Rooting out the negativity in your life, wherever it manifests itself (work, money and relationships are three of the most common causes), is key to securing your long-term happiness, so with each new piece of negativity you encounter, employ an extra tightening twist, tightening the tap, and tightening your grip on protecting your happiness.

TOP UP YOUR WATER COOLER

As lyricist Johnny Mercer wrote, for the famous Harold Arlen song, 'You've got to accentuate the positive, eliminate the negative'. The two, of course, go hand in hand, and by eliminating the negativity in your life you will be creating space for positivity; equally, by focusing on the positive aspects of your life you will be leaving less room for any negativity to creep in. So try to follow the advice of the song by using the following method:

First, list all the things in your life that are positive, no matter how large or small. Focus on them and see how they could be improved or expanded/extended. Try to imagine other ways you could accentuate the positivity, or bring in fresh positivity to your life.

Second, list all the things in your life that are negative, again no matter how large or small. Then work out how to combat them, to minimize their impact or, better still, to eliminate them altogether.

One important facet of doing this is that by getting all the negativity out into the open you can ensure that there is none that remains unseen, lurking to trip you up at an unexpected moment, and, crucially, that you don't allow yourself to dwell on any of it. It will also help you to keep track of the balance between the positivity and the negativity in your life, so that you are well placed to rectify it as soon as any negativity shows itself, and before it can take root.

KNOW YOUR TAP

In order to effectively combat any negativity, it is imperative that you are clear as to what constitutes such negativity. This may sound rather obvious, but in fact it is not; a good example of this is stress. This can be either positive or negative, or indeed both at the same time, and you will need to continually evaluate your situation to gain an insight into not just how much stress there is, and where it is coming from, but the ways in which it impacts your life. Only by doing this, not only for stress but for anything that is not clear cut as to its negativity or positivity in your life, can you see what changes you might need to make to your life.

One important fact to remember is that it is easy to become falsely negative through adopting an inappropriate set of criteria as your benchmark for success. It is commonplace to feel negative about your situation by allowing yourself to believe that you haven't achieved as much as you should have done by any given point. It is easy to fall into the trap of thinking that you should have achieved more, should own more, should be more – but this is only valid if you are not setting yourself a falsely high benchmark to begin with, and this has become increasingly difficult to get right with the rise of celebrity culture. Provided that you are not setting your standards too low, then self-acceptance is the key.

Putting it all together

Negativity, of any kind, is a damaging drain on your ability to be happy, while any and all positivity will help to bolster your happiness. Working out what exactly constitutes negativity in your life, where it is occurring and how to deal with it, is key to eradicating it and making room for the positive aspects of your life. For this reason, it should be done on a regular basis, and frequently – think of it as damage limitation to your happiness. By steering a path around as much of the negativity as it is possible to avoid, and by ensuring that you build in sufficient time and devote the necessary resources to auditing your situation and dealing with any negativity that cannot be avoided, boosting the positivity in your life, you will give yourself the necessary platform on which to build to achieve a long, lasting happiness.

21 Actively promoting passive positivity

> 'Once you replace negative thoughts with positive ones, you'll start having positive results.' Willie Nelson

> 'Few things in the world are more powerful than a positive push. A smile. A world of optimism and hope. A "you can do it" when things are tough.' Richard M. DeVos

> 'There is little difference in people, but that little difference makes a big difference. That little difference is attitude. The big difference is whether it is positive or negative.' Robert Collier

> 'But I have found that in the simple act of living with hope, and in the daily effort to have a positive impact in the world, the days I do have are made all the more meaningful and precious. And for that I am grateful.' Elizabeth Edwards

> 'You must not under any pretence allow your mind to dwell on any thought that is not positive, constructive, optimistic, kind.' Emmet Fox

In 2008, five entrepreneurs decided that if they could just gather together a large group of likeminded individuals, the creative energy that would be produced would be enormously powerful, and that the relationships formed would allow the creation of untold possibilities. They called the succession of meetings they developed the Summit Series, and the endeavour was successful right from the start.

In 2009, just one year after it launched, officials at the White House extended them an invitation to attend a gathering of senior officials and some of the most promising entrepreneurs. By the following year, the event had grown to include some 750 delegates, among them media mogul Ted Turner and former US president Bill Clinton (who said of the organization: 'What you're doing is a tremendous gift to the United States and to the world.').

Then in 2011 they chartered a cruise ship to host their inaugural Summit at Sea conference, where 1,000 entrepreneurs enjoyed three days sailing in the Bahamas, sharing their ideas and innovations – among the invitees were Sir Richard Branson, and Peter Thiel, the co-founder of PayPal. The original idea had snowballed, so successful had it proved to be, and yet the impetus was, in essence, so simple – to get together positive people, within a positive environment, and encourage them to help each other. This truly was proof positive of the power of positivity.

YOU ARE YOUR ENVIRONMENT

There is a Bantu concept, popularized by the late Nelson Mandela, which roughly translates as: 'I am who I am because of who we all are.' The need to surround yourself with positive people cannot be overstated in the quest for happiness; nor can the need to do away with the company of negative people who pull you down, whether intentionally or not.

Your environment, and particularly the people with whom you surround yourself, almost inevitably influence you more than you might imagine – and probably more than you would care to believe.

Naturally, you will find yourself surrounded by a variety of people in your life, some of whom are positive and encouraging, while others have just the opposite effect, radiating negativity and draining you of energy. Your wellbeing is greatly influenced by those around you, even to the point of picking up on their 'vibes' (energy and mood) without meaning to, and without anything being overtly communicated. So it is vital to make sure that those with whom you come into regular contact are positive people, people who will give you energy and encouragement, and quite simply make you happy.

Take the time to reflect how other people make you feel, in order to see what sort of effect they are having on your ability to be happy. If they are a positive influence be sure to tell them so, and try to spend more time with them. If they are a negative influence then be even surer to tell them so, and spend less time with them if their habits don't change.

The more candid you are about your own feelings and the way that certain people make you feel, the more honest you are likely to be when you tell others how they make you feel.

PERMANENTLY POSITIVE

Positivity is a constant boost to your happiness, and to other people's. Tell someone that they're beautiful and intelligent, and keep reinforcing it all the time, and before long they will believe it and their abilities will flourish as a result, as will their happiness. Keep telling the same person that they're ugly and stupid and the opposite will apply. So creating and maintaining a positive environment, and an attitude of positivity and optimism in your life, is essential in order to be happy.

Surround yourself with positivity (people, attitudes, successes, a feeling of optimism, etc.) and you will be happier simply by doing so. And while it is true that you cannot avoid experiencing any negativity in your life, you can avoid dwelling on it. Experience it, recognize it for what it is, and quickly move on.

Try thinking of your happiness as a large bowl, and any negativity that affects it as dirty water filling it up. The more dirty water you let in, the unhappier you will be. At the foot of the bowl there is a tap – turn it on and the dirty water can escape, gradually emptying the bowl. In order to be as happy as possible you will need to keep the bowl from filling up with all the negative, dirty water, since problems only occur once the bowl is completely filled and the water is allowed to overflow. So, clearly, you need to keep the rate at which water is leaving the bowl higher than the rate at which it is filling the bowl in order to be happy. But there is another, fundamental thing you can do to aid your cause, and that is to increase the size of your bowl. Simply put, the larger your bowl the more unhappiness can come your way before it affects you, and the size of your bowl is dictated by the amount of positivity you allow into your life, both your own and that provided by the people with whom you surround yourself.

SURROUND YOURSELF WITH POSITIVE PEOPLE

The entrepreneur and self-styled explorer Scott Dinsmore once said: 'I prioritize my life around spending time with passionate people… I spend time around passionate folks I don't even know, almost daily, because I seek out environments where they'll be… Spending time with them… is like therapy. (They) make me want to build new things, run faster, eat healthier, dream bigger and live on a new level altogether."

The influence of other people's outlook on life, and whether they make you feel positive and empowered or negative and depressed, can greatly affect your own life, and your ability to be happy. When you surround yourself with positive people, the negativity disappears leaving room for positivity, energy and feelings of wellbeing, and by spending time in the company of positive people you will feel yourself being empowered and optimistic. So choose your friends with care, for they create the environment in which you live. As the Greek philosopher Plato once put it: 'People are like dirt. They can either nourish you and help you grow as a person, or they can stunt your growth and make you wilt and die.'

Putting it all together

By surrounding yourself with positive people, and limiting, as much as possible, your access to anyone who is negative, your happiness will be greatly improved as you feed off their positivity and their positive energy. Positive environments and experiences work in much the same way. Try to seek out the places where positive people gather, and try to add your own positivity to the mix. In this way, not only will you benefit from the positivity of others, but you will also be giving something back, which in its own way creates a sense of happiness for you.

While it is true that you cannot avoid experiencing anything negative in your life, you can avoid dwelling on negative experiences. Remember that all the time you spend feeling negative is time wasted, whereas all the time you spend feeling positive is time well spent. Positivity is a direct and obvious bedfellow to happiness, and in the quest for maximizing your happiness you should look to maximize your positivity too.

22 The godsend you come to hate

9
10
11
12
13
14
15
16
17
18
19
20
21
22
23
24
25
26
27
28
29
30
31
32
33
34
35
36
37
38
39
40
41
42
43
44
45
46
47
48
49
50

> 'All of the books in the world contain no more information than is broadcast as video in a single large American city in a single year. Not all bits have equal value.' Carl Sagan

> 'Everybody gets so much information all day long that they lose their common sense.' Gertrude Stein

> 'Technological progress has merely provided us with more efficient means for going backwards.' Aldous Huxley

> 'The march of science and technology does not imply growing intellectual complexity in the lives of most people. It often means the opposite.' Thomas Sowell

> 'It has become appallingly obvious that our technology has exceeded our humanity.' Albert Einstein

After a considerable period of ignoring much of the available wealth of connectivity technology, and social media outlets, Chris decided to take the plunge and dive in. He got himself fixed up with everything that was available, and for a while he was like a kid in a sweetshop, relishing the abundance of ways that he could keep in touch with his friends, and with what was going on in the world. After a while, though, Chris realized that he was becoming less and less happy. At first he couldn't quite determine the cause, but it gradually dawned on him that he was now perpetually anxious, and he set about finding out why. Nothing had changed significantly in his life in recent months, except his decision to embrace all the latest technology and ways of keeping in touch, so he concentrated his efforts there – and it wasn't long before he discovered the cause. He had more than 400 'friends' on Facebook, even though he only actually knew just a handful of them, and he realized that he was worried if he didn't keep track of everything that was being posted in case he missed something; added to which was the fact that some of the posts were downright depressing, while many of the others were simply banal, and it irked him that it was wasting so much of his time wading through it all several times every day.

He also received constant streams of information from a variety of sources, the vast majority of which he didn't want, causing him to waste more time, and again making him unhappy. Then he felt an obligation to post regular tweets, since he had somehow accrued quite a number of followers on Twitter, and he felt under pressure to keep his blog up to date, and to always have something new and interesting to say. Then there were the texts, and calls, and instant messages that kept interrupting his life, and over which he felt he had little control. And so it went on. The only solution, he decided, was to cut out the vast majority of it, and he set about paring it right down to the minimum, leaving only those things which he knew he could control, and would enjoy. And suddenly he felt liberated, with the depressing weight of a large burden lifted, and his happiness returned to its former level, and then a little higher, as he became truly able to make the new technology work for him.

LIMIT OTHER PEOPLE'S ACCESS TO YOU

When it comes to providing happiness, technology can be both a blessing and a curse – and often at the same time! One of the challenges it provides is that unless you are careful to limit the amount of access you have to the various types of technology, it can start to take over your life. In today's always-on, always connected world, it can be difficult to find any real downtime, and the long-term effects of being permanently on the go are damaging to your happiness. It is vital that you find moments in your life where you can totally relax, and this means completely switching off, both mentally and literally. If you've never tried it (and many people haven't), then find a time to do just that – switch off all the technology that keeps you in never-ending communication with the world, including your mobile phone and landline, your television,

computers, laptops and tablets, your Blackberry and consoles –
everything that can interrupt your life, and which in all likelihood
frequently does so. Then sit back to enjoy the peace.

Tellingly, many people find this an unnerving experience, even if
they only try it for a short while. The silence can be deafening,
and the sense of being off the radar can leave people feeling
wary, even nervous. But persevere and you'll undergo an
experience that is wonderfully freeing, as if a large weight is being
lifted from your shoulders; without the constant interruptions
with which you are usually faced you can devote your attention
to complete relaxation, a must for anyone wishing to maximize
their happiness. Not only this, but the very fact of knowing that
people can't reach you, whether or not they would have done, is
in itself an incredibly liberating experience.

LIMIT YOUR ACCESS TO OTHER PEOPLE

In the same way, if you are to maximize your happiness it is
important that you determine how much access to other people,
and to the information and connectivity overload that awaits
you permanently on the other side of your technology if it is
not diligently controlled, really makes you happy. How often do
you see people texting, playing games on their phone or tablet,
searching out their friends through Facebook or Twitter or the like,
instead of communicating in the real world? And how often is that
person you?! It is not, of course, that technology is a bad thing –
quite the opposite, in fact. Used appropriately, it can be wonderful,
allowing a level of communication never before imagined, and
giving access to myriad leisure pursuits quickly, easily and wherever
and whenever you want them and connecting people who might
otherwise be isolated or lonely. But take your eye off the ball and
it can quickly threaten to overwhelm you, until you get to the
point where you feel uneasy when you are not checking every five
minutes for the latest updates from favourite websites, from news
feeds, from social media and the like. When it gets to this point it
has become an addiction, and no form of addiction can be healthy,
so technology has become a barrier to happiness. By controlling
the technology you use, and not allowing it to dictate its terms
to you, it can be utilized in ways that make you happier, without
risking any side effects that are detrimental to your happiness.

CHOOSE YOUR TECHNOLOGY CAREFULLY

Making technology work for you is largely a matter of selecting the right technology in the first place. This means avoiding the temptation to simply jump on the technology bandwagon, since this can quickly threaten to overwhelm, and even enslave you, such is the wealth of technology available. But it's not just the technology – it's the access it gives you to the wider world, and the access it gives the wider world to you; access that can be liberating and fun, but which can just as easily be suffocating and anxiety-provoking if it is not controlled. It can even be isolating, leading to loneliness, if it is allowed to take over too much of your life, since the virtual contact it provides can never replace real-world contact, and of course such an outcome can only be detrimental to your happiness.

Choose the right technology for you, however, and keep a careful eye on how – and how often – you are using it, and it can add significantly to your happiness. The best approach is to work from the ground up. In other words, avoid the temptation to see what technology is available and just start using it, and instead determine first of all what the various technologies can give you that you are currently lacking, and which will add to your happiness in some way. By taking this approach you will limit your use of technology to that which will actively increase your happiness, without threatening to become a negative influence on your life. And since most people already use a good deal of technology every day, making sure that its contribution to your life is always positive is a great way to quickly add to your happiness. Be sure to carry out regular reviews so that you don't start to slide, allowing new ways of wasting your time to creep in unnoticed, or adding to your worries, or otherwise making you less happy.

Putting it all together

It is crucial, in the pursuit of happiness, that you discover the ways in which you can make technology work for you, by mastering those elements that make a positive contribution to your life, and by eliminating all those that don't, or which threaten to overwhelm you; failing to put in place the appropriate safeguards is a short cut to unnecessary stress and anxiety. Technology, used appropriately, can add significantly to your happiness, simplifying otherwise complicated tasks (which only make your life unnecessarily complicated and get in the way of your happiness), allowing easy and immediate connectivity, and providing a conduit to leisure pursuits. Used inappropriately, however, it can quickly and effectively erode your happiness.

It is crucial that you keep a constant watch on the ways in which technology impacts on your life, and on your happiness, since its effects occur gradually, building up over time, and without careful monitoring they can easily slip in under the radar. One of the ways in which today's technology can unwittingly become a burden is that it can create a persistent anxiety that you may be missing out on something if you are not checking it every two minutes. Even if you enjoy the constant connection technology affords, it is important to sometimes disconnect yourself from it, in order to enjoy a level of freedom that is otherwise impossible; and if the thought of doing so worries you, then it is doubly important.

23 Your future happiness lies in the past

" *'For my part, I consider that it will be found much better by all parties to leave the past to history, especially as I propose to write that history myself.'* Winston Churchill

" *'Who controls the past controls the future. Who controls the present controls the past.'* George Orwell

" *'The only difference between the saint and the sinner is that every saint has a past, and every sinner has a future.'* Oscar Wilde

" *'Pick the day. Enjoy it – to the hilt. The day as it comes. People as they come… The past, I think, has helped me appreciate the present – and I don't want to spoil any of it by fretting about the future.'* Audrey Hepburn

" *'I don't like nostalgia unless it's mine.'* Lou Reed

A newly ordained priest was given his first parish, and after a few months the bishop of the diocese, who was notorious for his bad memory, decided to pay him a visit. He was impressed with the young man's charisma, and it was clear that his parishioners had taken to him. On the Sunday, the bishop and the young priest celebrated mass together, and when it came to the sermon the young priest stood in the pulpit, cleared his throat and, looking solemnly at his congregation, said: 'Dear parishioners, I have a confession to make to you all.' They were instantly silent and attentive, curious and alarmed to hear what he would say. The young priest continued: 'I must tell you that some of the happiest moments of my life have been spent in the arms of another man's wife.' A collective gasp echoed through the church, and the bishop's jaw dropped open, unable to believe what he was hearing. After an awkward moment that seemed to last forever the young priest broke into a grin and continued: 'I am, of course, referring to my mother.'

The parishioners were delighted with the ruse, and the bishop grinned broadly, admiring the young man's technique, for now he had them in the palm of his hand. After the mass the bishop congratulated the priest, and asked him if he would mind if he borrowed the joke the following weekend, when he was due to address the Women's Guild. The young priest was flattered, and delighted that the bishop would be using his material, and so the following weekend, when the bishop was saying mass for all the ladies of the Women's Guild, he approach the pulpit with a twinkle in his eye, looked gravely at his congregation, and said: 'Ladies, I have a confession to make to you all. I must tell you that some of the happiest moments of my life have been spent in the arms of another man's wife.' They were shocked, and fell immediately silent. Then the bishop broke into a mischievous grin before looking slightly puzzled, then concerned. 'And for the life of me,' he continued, 'I can't remember who she was.'

Taking a moment to capture the details of enjoyable events and occasions, and significant moments, can be an important resource in your quest to be happy, since they will form the backbone of your store of 'feel good' memories to enjoy in the future. Just remember that these memories are only as good – and therefore as useful to you – as your memory!

GO FOR IT

It is said that you always regret the things you haven't done more than the things you have; though, obviously, that does depend on the nature of the things in question! But the general premise is certainly true, that it is easier to live with the mistakes you might make while trying to reach a goal, or pursue an activity or dream, than it is to settle for the knowledge that you never tried. So don't be afraid to seize the opportunities that come your way, and even to create the ones that don't – just be sure that you go into each clear in the understanding of what you hope to get out of them, and the ways in which you think they will make you happy. Then if they do, that's brilliant, mission accomplished, and even if they don't, at least you won't have to live with the unsettling regret that you didn't even try.

YOUR EXPERIENCES, YOURSELF

Over the course of your lifetime your personality, and your outlook on life, are shaped by your experiences. The people you meet, the things you do, the places you go – all have a direct bearing on who you will be in the future. And this relates directly to your ability to be happy in the future, since you will decide, by selecting the course you take through life, how you react to whatever situations occur further down the line. Will you be someone who is positive, optimistic and quick to be happy, or will you be someone whose glass is always half empty, and who never seems to be happy unless they are miserable? This does also depend upon your natural inclinations, of course, but it is largely down to the way you shape your life, and even those predisposed to seeing the worst in each situation can, over time, learn to always look for the best. So try to ensure that you keep a positive outlook on life, whatever you do, and that you are always quick to seize any opportunity to experience something that might make you happy, and that even if it doesn't, you don't allow yourself to wallow in self-pity, but instead take what positives you can from it and move on, with a renewed optimism for the future.

'MENTAL SCRAPBOOKING'

Collecting memories from a wealth of experiences throughout your life is a great way to ensure that you have a store of positive and enjoyable 'rocking chair' moments to look back on in the years to come. Just as you would put aside money to shield you from future misfortune, so having positive experiences and collecting the memories that go with them is a way of investing in your future happiness. It is also a great way to gain extra pleasure from the experiences as they happen, and directly afterwards, since ensuring that you remember them accurately means taking a greater interest in them as they occur. Of course this strategy is only useful provided that you can remember the events in years to come! To this end, you will need to develop a way of committing them to memory.

'Mental scrapbooking' is one of the best ways to do this, and involves taking a mental snapshot of the occasion or, better still, a series of mental snapshots, and labelling each one so that you can remember the event in as much detail as possible in years to come. Imagine creating a scrapbook in the traditional sense – documenting moments or events by taking pictures, and writing captions to go with them, maybe adding a ticket or receipt from an event, or a particular phrase someone used at the time – whatever will aid your memory in the future. Remember, though, that this doesn't have to make sense to anyone else, so you don't need to try to explain everything; simply collect sufficient mental material to bring everything vividly back to life for you when you recall a particular situation.

You can also add physical aides-mémoires if they help, such as photographs, writing, objects, etc. – anything that will help you as you try to recall not only details of the events, but also the feelings that accompanied them. These, however, can tarnish over time, or even become mislaid – but your memories, properly catalogued, can stay fresh for as long as you need them, and you will always have them to hand.

Putting it all together

Creating 'rocking chair' moments gives you the opportunity to review your life's best moments, both directly after they occur, and in the future – and as often as you wish. Reminiscing about the best moments you've experienced is a great way to lift your mood quickly, and to motivate yourself to achieve more such moments in the future, to add to your bank of positive memories. In this way you can help to safeguard your future happiness by creating a repository of feelgood moments, which will help to shield you should you experience any sudden misfortune later in life. Remember that these are the very best moments in your life – events, occasions, achievements, etc. – of which you are proud, and which made you happy, so they can be relied upon to lighten your mood whenever you recall them. By creating a store of positivity in your life, and by surrounding yourself with positive people and positive occasions, you can create a bank of great memories to make you happy every time you recall them, now and in the future.

24 Your best today is tomorrow

>> 'A dream is your creative vision for your life in the future. You must break out of your current comfort zone and become comfortable with the unfamiliar and the unknown.' Denis Waitley

>> 'Let others lead small lives, but not you. Let others argue over small things, but not you. Let others cry over small hurts, but not you. Let others leave their future in someone else's hands, but not you.' Jim Rohn

>> 'We should regret our mistakes and learn from them, but never carry them forward into the future with us.' Lucy Maud Montgomery

>> 'The future belongs to those who prepare for it today.' Malcolm X

>> 'It is always wise to look ahead, but difficult to look further than you can see.' Winston Churchill

Sarah had a reasonable job, and lived in a reasonable house, in a reasonable town. In fact, everything about Sarah's life was reasonable – and that was what she found so depressing. It wasn't that there was anything particularly wrong with any part of her life. Sure, she experienced the usual niggles, with work, with her boyfriend, even with her hobbies, but that was to be expected, it was just a part and parcel of everyday life. On the whole, though, things were perfectly fine, but what was lacking was any real excitement. Sarah couldn't remember the last time she had had anything that was really worth looking forward to, anything about which just the thought of it filled her with the pleasure of excited anticipation. Sarah wondered if she should discuss it with Chris, her boyfriend, but she was nervous about how that conversation might go. Then it dawned on her that she was always anxious about how things might go, always avoiding anything where she might rock the boat for fear of the outcome, but as a result no one but Sarah knew what she really wanted from life, and so no one could help her get it.

After much deliberation she decided to bite the bullet and told Chris how she felt. To her great surprise and relief he told her that he felt the same way, and so they determined to do something about it. They immediately set about listing all the things they wanted to do in life: the things they wanted to achieve, the places they wanted to go, the experiences they wanted to have, the events they wanted to attend, as well as mapping their dreams. Suddenly they both felt as if a weight had been lifted from their shoulders, and they put in place a plan to ensure that every week they would have at least one thing that they could both look forward to. In addition, they set about researching each other's long-term dream. By doing this they both got a clearer understanding of what it was that their partner wanted, and also discovered some new information on the subject with which to surprise each other. They then set about finding ways to help each other experience their dream, if only in part, by doing something that would also give them an event to look forward to, and which would help to put flesh on the bones of their dream at the same time.

Chris's dream was to own a Ferrari, so Sarah booked tickets to a forthcoming car show at which she knew Ferrari would be exhibiting. Chris was delighted that he would get to see, and even sit in a Ferrari, and the trip would not only give him something to look forward to, but would help to flesh out the details of his long-term dream. Sarah's dream was to visit New Zealand, so Chris collected information on the islands from a variety of sources, and also collected some travel brochures that detailed holidays there. He also worked out how much they would have to save each week in order to turn Sarah's dream into a reality, and calculated that they would be able to afford it within three to four years. So a plan was immediately hatched, and Sarah definitely had something about which to be excited every single day.

PAINTING YOUR DREAM

It is important to always have something to look forward to, no matter how large or small, since joyful anticipation will always brighten your mood, whatever else may be happening in your life. By ensuring that you have a definite and tangible event or occasion about which you are excited, you will always have at your disposal something to which you can turn your mind when the going gets tough, something to lift your spirits and bring you happiness. Since the only thing you need to lift your spirits in this way is the thought of what awaits you, without the complicated baggage of determining exactly how it will all work or how it will pan out, you can paint your vision to the very best effect, creating in your imagination the most perfect outcome, and without the hindrance of reality getting in the way!

So why not paint your dream? Your vision of a perfect future can be as simple or as full as you want to make it. Perhaps it is owning your dream car, or taking your dream holiday; or maybe you like to imagine your ideal house, picturing in detail each room and what you would use them for, how you would decorate them, etc. Your dream might even be a business you want to get off the ground; perhaps you want to be your own boss, and this may involve a hugely detailed plan. Whatever your dream is, though, it is important that you paint it in your mind's eye in as much detail as possible, so that it becomes for you as real as possible. In this way, whenever you call it to mind, it will be strikingly vivid, and the very thought of it will provide an immediate boost to your happiness.

START WITH BABY STEPS

We have already seen that it can be very beneficial to paint your dream of the future, but it is also useful to have at your constant disposal some smaller events or occasions that will lift your mood, and which are more immediate. They too need to be described in as much detail as possible in order to provide the maximum benefit and, since they are things that lie not far off, this should be fairly easy to accomplish.

Perhaps you are going to a concert, a party, a sporting event or the theatre, and it is an outing you are really looking forward to.

Try thinking through what exactly the occasion might provide, and be sure to keep at bay any reality checks since the purpose of this is to raise your spirits, and not to provide a detailed plan of the event. So if it is a sporting occasion, picture your team winning; if it is a trip to the theatre, imagine seeing the finest performances and the most lavish sets and costumes, and so on. Don't be concerned that you are merely setting yourself up for disappointment later on, since events rarely play themselves out exactly as we may have anticipated. Instead, revel in the joy that imagining a perfect outcome affords you, and enjoy the benefits brought by this instant tonic.

YOUR CONSTANT COMPANION

One of the great benefits of excited anticipation about a forthcoming event or occasion is that you carry it with you wherever you go. Without any effort on your part it will always be with you, your constant companion and ever reliable mood lifter. Having short- , medium- and long-term dreams and targets (as well as desires of varying magnitudes, e.g. a tangible goal, something that would be great but is perhaps less likely, and your ultimate dream) means that you can quickly and easily cover all bases so that wherever you are, whatever you are doing and whatever mood this puts you in, you can be sure of always having at your disposal something to lift your spirits. The more detail in which you can imagine them, the more useful they will prove to be, and by having in mind what they are, and how you imagine them to play out, you can call on them at any time to help you to stay cheerful, whatever the circumstances.

Putting it all together

Anticipation of an enjoyable event or occasion is a guaranteed and quick-fire way to lift your mood. By thinking of a forthcoming scenario to which you are looking forward, and imagining for it a perfect outcome, and in as much detail as possible, you can lift your spirits and give your happiness a boost whenever and wherever you need to. And by painting your long-term vision of a perfect future, or simply by imagining that one item or occasion with which you would spoil yourself if you could, you will have this weapon in your arsenal even if you don't have any enjoyable events lined up in the near future. Since all that is required to enjoy the happiness boost this strategy provides is your imagination, you will always have it at your disposal, and it can be called upon at a moment's notice. Not only that, but you can revisit it as often as you like, and even revise it and improve it as you go along. With careful planning you can give yourself the best possible chance of always having something to look forward to, and you can give yourself a challenge to try to ensure that each day contains more, and better, happy moments than the last. In this way you can end each day happier than you began it, and begin each day happier than you began the last.

25 So you think your life sucks?

❝ *'Don't ever criticize yourself. Don't go around all day long thinking, "I'm unattractive, I'm slow, I'm not as smart as my brother". God wasn't having a bad day when he made you... If you don't love yourself in the right way, you can't love your neighbour. You can't be as good as you are supposed to be.'* Joel Osteen

❝ *'Review your goals twice every day in order to be focused on achieving them.'* Les Brown

❝ *'Even your most talented employees have room for growth in some area, and you're doing your employee a disservice if the sum of your review is: "You're great!" No matter how talented the employee, think of ways he could grow towards the position he might want to hold two, five, or ten years down the line.'* Kathryn Minshew

❝ *'When a man stops dreaming, he stops hoping; but when he learns to dream realistically, he starts living.'* David Wyndham

❝ *'I spent a good deal of time going back over my childhood, my midlife, to try to understand who I was. We're supposed to be complete and whole, and you can't be whole if you're trying to be perfect. Doing a life review helped me get over the disease to please.'* Jane Fonda

When, in 1888, Alfred Nobel's brother, Ludvig, died while visiting Cannes, a local newspaper heard of the tragic event but mistakenly understood it to have been Alfred whose health had failed. They immediately printed his obituary, and it was a less-than-flattering portrait of the man. Indeed, to Alfred it was to prove to be a real wake-up call. 'Le marchand de la mort est mort,' ('The merchant of death is dead') averred the article, going on to say that his primary accomplishment was to discover ever-greater methods of killing more people, faster.

Upon reading it, and concerned with his legacy, and the way that history would remember him, Alfred Nobel determined to devote the vast majority of his sizeable fortune, gained through the research, development and production of dynamite, to establishing five awards in his name, to be presented each year to those who were deemed to have done great things to bring about positive change in the world.

More than a century later the awards (now numbering six for Chemistry, Physics, Peace, Economics, Medicine and Literature) are still being presented, and Nobel Prizes are a by-word for excellence in a number of fields. Yet without the erroneous and harsh obituary, which prompted Alfred Nobel to reflect on his life and legacy, they would probably never have existed at all.

WHAT NEEDS TO CHANGE?

However happy, or otherwise, you feel you are, there is almost always room for improvement. By carrying out periodic reviews of your happiness, you will be able to determine just how happy you are with your life, and what, if anything, needs to change. And the chances are that something will need to change, or at least that you will benefit in some way from any changes you may decide to make.

In order to make such a review as useful as possible, it needs to be as rigorous as possible. How often you carry out such a review will depend on how often you feel your circumstances change, but it is best not to leave it too long or you may find that valuable time has elapsed during which you were not as happy as you might have been. The review need not be onerous, nor take too much of your time, and the more often you carry it out, the quicker you will become at doing so.

Try to allocate a time when you will not be interrupted, and commit to paper the key elements of your life, determining which are, and which are not, making you happy. Obviously, those that are making you unhappy require change, but just as important is a review of whether or not those things that are making you happy, are actually making you as happy as they should.

By carrying out regular life reviews you will quickly be able to determine how and where you can improve your happiness, and you will also have at your disposal an easy means of highlighting those areas that are ripe for change.

FUNDAMENTAL CHANGES

Determining the fundamental changes you need to make in your life and how the changes can bring you greater happiness is vital to effect lasting change. These are the most important changes you need to identify in your regular happiness reviews – those things that affect, either directly or indirectly, the fundamental aspects of your life and that have a direct impact on your happiness. They are the changes you should prioritize, since they are the changes that will have the greatest effect on your happiness.

Unfortunately, they are often the changes that are the most difficult to implement, and which take the longest time and the most effort. The key is to identify just how fundamental to your happiness the changes you make will be. In other words, will it be worth all the effort once it is done? If it will, then clearly it is something worth doing, but if it is something that will be a chore to get underway, you will need to put the 'fun' back into fundamental.

Try to break the task down into manageable chunks, and to always have in mind the benefits to your happiness that the changes will make. Then review the changes as you make them, to make sure that they are bringing you the benefits you expected.

CHANGE FOR CHANGE'S SAKE

There is no point in making changes just for the sake of it, since this will cost you time and effort, depleting your resources which could be used more beneficially elsewhere. However, there is certainly a point in making changes to things that are not necessarily making you unhappy, but which you have identified as areas that could be bringing you more happiness than they currently are.

A useful exercise is to think about the five things in your life that you would change if you could. What are the changes you need to make? And how can you bring about the changes? Remember that the changes can be large or small, provided that they will significantly improve your happiness. Indeed, it is sometimes tiny, incremental changes made to areas where we are already happy that bring us the most additional happiness. So do not disregard anything, no matter how insignificant it may seem, provided that you are not simply making a change for change's sake, but that the changes you make really will improve your happiness.

Putting it all together

Undertaking periodic reviews of your situation, in order to determine your level of happiness, is a vital tool in helping you to understand how and where improvements can be made, and also in highlighting those areas that are currently making you unhappy.

Make sure that you set aside sufficient quality time to carry out a quality review, and that once you have identified changes that need to be made, you put in place a strategy and timeframe for implementing them. They should not be simply changes for the sake of them, but neither do they need to be wholesale changes. What matters is not the size of the changes that are made, but the degree to which they will improve your happiness once completed.

If your resources are limited, be sure that you have identified the most fundamental changes that need to be made, and start with these. By developing and executing strategies for implementing the changes you can be sure that they really will happen, and in a timely manner, and that your happiness will directly benefit as a result.

26 Enjoy the things you hate

‘I like to make the mundane fabulous whenever I can.’
Rufus Wainwright

‘I would sum up my fear about the future in one word: boring. And that's my one fear: that everything has happened; nothing exciting or new or interesting is ever going to happen again… the future is just going to be a vast, conforming suburb of the soul.’ J. G. Ballard

‘There's something that's really fun about the challenge of making the mundane funny, too, I think.’ Jim Gaffigan

‘If you knew that your life was merely a phase or short, short segment of your entire existence, how would you live? Knowing nothing "real" was at risk, what would you do? You'd live a gigantic, bold, fun, dazzling life. You know you would. That's what the ghosts want us to do — all the exciting things they no longer can.’ Chuck Palahniuk

‘Life is intrinsically, well, boring and dangerous at the same time. At any given moment the floor may open up. Of course, it almost never does; that's what makes it so boring.’ Edward Gorey

Barry awoke to the stark realization that he was dying. Not physically, but in every other way, little by little, he was being eroded. It wasn't his work that was killing him — far from it, his job was ridiculously easy and mundane and monotonous. It wasn't his home life, which was a grey, dull nothing. It wasn't the numbing boredom of the commute, or any other single aspect of his beige existence. It was all of them. Separately, he could cope, but it was the cumulative effect of them all together. He could tolerate one or two parts of his life being boring, but not all of it. Every aspect of every day of Barry's life was mindless and tedious, until one day he realized that he needed to shake things up, and drastically, or there might be no coming back from the brink.

But what could he change? His job, as much as he disliked it, paid the bills, and he really wasn't qualified to do much else. Equally, he didn't think it was likely that he could improve his life elsewhere very easily. So he decided to start with small steps. He bought himself an audio book to listen to during his commute, and from the very first day he was hooked. Suddenly the half an hour he spent in traffic at the start and end of each day was something to be looked forward to, not dreaded as it always had been. Inspired, he decided to listen to the radio while doing his laundry. He very nearly gave it up as a bad idea as there was nothing on that caught his interest, until it dawned on him to schedule this most boring of tasks for a time when there was something worth listening to. It worked, and another tedious activity was made more fun. In fact, Barry decided that in order to listen to all the radio programmes he wanted to, he would start cooking himself proper meals instead of relying on ready meals and takeaways. He began looking forward to ironing, too, and to cleaning. To make the weekly grocery shop fun he spent the time thinking of all the lovely meals he would enjoy, and playing word games with the names of the products. Before long, Barry had turned every activity he had dreaded into something to be relished, and his mundane existence into something enjoyable and fruitful.

CONQUERING THE MUNDANE

Life – everybody's life – is full of the mundane, the ordinary and the boring. Even those people whose lives we think must be fabulously exciting are usually bogged down in unglamorous, but necessary, everyday tasks. In fact, it is true to say that the majority of our lives is taken up with things that could be considered to be mundane. So in the quest to maximize our happiness, it is imperative that we find a way to conquer the mundane, and turn it to our advantage. It is unlikely, of course, that you will find ways to make doing the laundry, the washing up or mowing the lawn the most exciting parts of your day! But of course they don't need to be exciting to be enjoyable, and they need only be enjoyable in order to make you happy. And the more ordinary tasks you can transform into something which you can enjoy, the more of your life you will spend being happy. Indeed, since so much of our lives is taken up with mundane everyday tasks, finding ways to enjoy them is crucial in the quest to maximize your happiness.

One of the best ways to achieve this is to combine something you enjoy with something you don't, for instance listening to the radio while ironing, or planning your next holiday while doing the laundry. In this way, the mundane tasks can pass almost unnoticed, replaced by something you enjoy, and a large part of your life, which could otherwise have brought you down with its drudgery, can be transformed into something that makes you happy.

PUTTING THE 'FUN' BACK INTO FUNDAMENTAL

Finding ways of making even the most mundane tasks fun is an important part of the process of maximizing your happiness. By developing creative ways of overcoming, or reframing, the unavoidable but boring elements of your life so that you actually look forward to them, and even learn to love doing them, you can dramatically transform a large part of your life. Trying to avoid life's less glamorous and exciting but nonetheless fundamental aspects is a mug's game, since it almost inevitably leads to prevarication and procrastination. In other words, the boring parts of your everyday life cannot be avoided, they can only be postponed. It is far better, then, not to delay them (which doesn't get them out of your hair anyway and simply leaves them hanging over you, a depressing thought whenever you are reminded of them), but to tackle them head-on, and to do so in such a way as to make them fun.

The most important factor in achieving this is that you don't need any external stimulus to make it happen. Your imagination, and your anticipation of future, enjoyable events is all that is required – that, and remembering to do it! The next time you find yourself faced with a mundane task, make a conscious effort to spend the time either anticipating some future event or occasion to which you are looking forward, or else to allow your imagination to wander anywhere that will make you happy. And if you complete a mundane task and realize that you haven't spent the time in enjoyable thoughts, try finding a way to trigger them the next time around.

COLOUR YOUR HAPPINESS

Which colours make you the happiest? Red? Blue? Pink? Yellow? Whichever they are, two colours that are unlikely to feature are grey and beige. Yet so much of our day-to-day lives is grey or beige, and unavoidably so, as we go about doing all the things that we have to do, but which don't exactly fill our lives with excitement. So is it a dead loss, or is there a way to turn the beige into stunning blues and the grey into vibrant greens? We have already seen that spending the time engaged in a more enjoyable stimulus, and using your imagination or planning for enjoyable future events, are two ways to transform mundane tasks into enjoyable periods. The next step is to take them to the next level, by transforming gentle enjoyment into acute pleasure. There is no magic trick to this, it is simply a matter of practice, but by getting into the habit of using this strategy every time you're faced with a mundane task, you will soon find that your ability to make it work to your advantage steadily improves, until the point where previously mundane tasks no longer seem mundane, and can even become enjoyable events in their own right.

Putting it all together

It is impossible to escape the mundane but necessary tasks that we are faced with every day, but it is possible to transform them into occasions that make us happy. By changing our mindset so that we no longer view mundane tasks as boring, but instead begin to see them as occasions we can enjoy, and which can make us happy, we can both eradicate events that might otherwise have threatened our good mood and, at the same time, create new instances of enjoyment. Trying to stem the tide of boring tasks in your life is rather like trying to push a pebble uphill with your nose! You can sustain it for a while, but it is impossible to get very far, and when you look back at your efforts you will probably wonder why you ever tried in the first place. Instead, it is far better to accept the inevitable, but turn the inevitable to your advantage, by transforming the mundane, everyday tasks in your life into occasions to be looked forward to, savoured and even looked back on with fondness.

27 Your happiness, your problem

> **''** 'No problem can be solved from the same level of consciousness that created it.' Albert Einstein

> **''** 'The best way of removing negativity is to laugh and be joyous.' David Icke

> **''** 'Happiness is when what you think, what you say, and what you do are in harmony.' Mohandas K. Gandhi

> **''** 'If you want others to be happy, practise compassion. If you want to be happy, practise compassion.' Dalai Lama

> **''** 'All progress is precarious, and the solution of one problem brings us face to face with another problem.' Martin Luther King, Jr

A man decided to visit his doctor, on an errand of some delicacy.

'And what can I do for you?' enquired the doctor.

The man looked uneasy, and confided that he and his wife had not been able to have the physical relationship they used to enjoy. 'We always loved having sex,' he said, 'but just recently it hasn't been happening for us. Is there anything you can do?'

The doctor was rather taken aback, given the appearance of the man, and hurriedly checked his notes, but he found that his first impression was indeed correct. 'Let me get this straight,' he said. 'You're telling me that you're not enjoying sex the way you used to, is that right?'

'That's it exactly,' confirmed the man.

'And would you say your wife feels the same way?' asked the doctor.

'Oh, absolutely yes,' said the man. 'It's such a pity; we used to enjoy it so much.'

'I see,' said the doctor. He leaned forward in his seat, and continued. 'Now look here,' he began, 'I don't wish to seem indelicate but do you mind if I ask you how old you are?'

'No, not at all,' replied the man. 'I'm eighty-nine.'

'Eighty-nine!' gasped the doctor incredulously. 'Eighty-nine! And how old is your wife?'

'Ninety-two,' said the man.

'Ninety-two!' echoed the doctor, scarcely able to believe his ears.

'That's right,' said the man.

'You mean to tell me that you're saying you and your wife are not enjoying sex as much as you used to,' the doctor went on, 'and that you are eighty-nine years old, and your wife is ninety-two?'

'Exactly,' confirmed the man.

The doctor was flabbergasted, thinking he'd heard it all now. 'And when exactly did you first notice this?' he asked.

The man thought for a moment before replying. 'Twice last night, and then again this morning!' he said.

Whatever happiness means for you, and whatever constitutes success in your life in terms of maximizing your happiness, that is what you need to focus on. Don't be misled by the needs and wants of others, for what makes them happy may not make you happy at all, and vice versa. So be true to yourself, and your requirements for happiness, and seek out as many opportunities as you can to experience the things that make you happiest.

YOUR HAPPINESS IS YOUR OWN

It is said that one man's meat is another man's poison, and this is certainly true when it comes to happiness. The things that make you joyful might have little impact for someone else, and the things that bring them peace and contentment might not feature on your radar at all. So finding out what makes you happy, and how to achieve it, is of paramount importance in the quest to finding ways to maximize your happiness. It is easy, and commonplace, to assume that happiness is the same for everyone, but this simply isn't the case. How we experience happiness, what it constitutes for us, and how we can best achieve it, differs from person to person; so too does the very experience of being happy, since it is an emotion that is experienced uniquely for each and every person.

To see this in action, try thinking of something that makes you blissfully content, and another thing that makes you ecstatic. Then try thinking of someone you know and whose personality and tastes are quite dissimilar to yours, and put them in these situations. Their responses to them are likely to differ markedly from yours, just as yours would if you were to experience situations that aroused in them the same responses of contentment or joy. And even the very experiences differ for each person – the way in which you experience joy, for instance, might be quite different to the way someone else experiences it, and the way it makes you feel may not be the same for another person. This is because there are so many factors that have to be taken into account that the chances of two people's experiences being exactly the same are slim, even though they will have similar responses, at least in broad terms. So identifying exactly what each type of happiness means for you, and how you experience it, is an important step in reaching maximum happiness.

DISCOVER YOUR HAPPINESS

Happiness is a common, shared emotion, but one that is experienced differently by everyone, and its causes and responses likewise vary widely. So what exactly does happiness mean for you, and how can you best experience it? You could be forgiven for assuming that you must automatically know the answer to this, since you must know what makes you happy, but one doesn't necessarily follow the other. You know that certain situations or events are likely to make you happy, but the type of happiness each will trigger, and whether one type will segue into another, or can be made to do so, can be more difficult to pin down. For instance, a situation that you anticipate will make you excited, such as attending a wedding, may in the event make you joyous and deeply content, but not excited. This is because there are so many variables to take into consideration that it is difficult to accurately predict your happiness response to any given situation. Even so, by being aware of the way a situation makes you feel, as opposed to just experiencing it subconsciously, you can maximize its benefits to you, and even learn to turn one sort of happiness into another.

EXPERIENCE UNIQUE HAPPINESS

There simply is no 'one size fits all' approach to happiness, and finding what works best for you may not be as straightforward as you might think. Yet how often are we guilty of trying to fit a square peg into a round hole? It is often assumed that what makes one person happy must make everyone happy, and as a result it is commonplace to find that you are expected to be happy under certain circumstances, even when you might not be. This isn't because you are not predisposed to being happy at that moment, but simply because the event or situation isn't one that will make you so.

Even more common is the experience of being expected to respond with a particular form of happiness, whereas what you actually feel is another kind. This can lead to awkward moments, and even to pretending that you feel something that you do not, but it is crucial to understand, and to be true to, your unique happiness triggers and responses. Only in this way can the emotions you experience be completely genuine, and only if they are genuine can they be experienced fully.

Putting it all together

Understanding what makes you happy, how it works, what the triggers are and how you will respond to them, is important in being able to maximize your happiness. Attending an event that someone else thinks will make you really excited, for instance, but which actually makes you deeply satisfied, will be compromised if you spend the whole time feeling awkward that you are expected to be excited, and can even end up making you feel guilty! Yet if you are able to just respond with whatever emotions you are genuinely feeling, you will be able to take advantage of a wonderful period of contentment. So knowing what makes you happy, and being confident to experience it in your own way, is a necessary skill to learn in order to ensure that you take full advantage of each and every occasion to be happy – in whatever way.

28 The ten kinds of happy – and how to find them

> 'There is no austerity equal to a balanced mind, and there is no happiness equal to contentment; there is no disease like covetousness, and no virtue like mercy.' Chanakya

> 'True happiness comes from the joy of deeds well done, the zest of creating things new.' Antoine de Saint-Exupéry

> 'When you are discontent, you always want more, more, more. Your desire can never be satisfied. But when you practise contentment, you can say to yourself, "Oh yes – I already have everything that I really need".' Dalai Lama

> 'Love is a force more formidable than any other. It is invisible – it cannot be seen or measured, yet it is powerful enough to transform you in a moment, and offer you more joy than any material possession could.' Barbara De Angelis

> 'The human mind is capable of excitement without the application of gross and violent stimulants; and he must have a very faint perception of its beauty and dignity who does not know this.' William Wordsworth

Linda thought she was happy. All those who knew her would have said the same. But one day, in conversation with someone at work, Linda began to get the uneasy feeling that her colleague was getting so much more out of life than she was. By listening to her friend's tales, Linda began to realize that although she was happy with her life, at least for the most part, she wasn't as happy as she could be, and that indeed there were whole swathes of her life in which she was simply missing out on happiness.

As Linda began to question the way she was living her life, she began to analyse how she could live it better; how she could squeeze more happiness from those things that currently made her happy and how she could find new and different ways to be happy.

Linda asked her colleague how she had gone about getting her life in such great shape. The answer, she was told, was that some time ago she had carried out a comprehensive review of her life, and that she had realized that although for the most part it was okay, she certainly wasn't anywhere near as happy as she thought she should have been – and could be.

She had therefore resolved to do something about it and had highlighted all the ways in which she felt she was missing out on happiness. Crucially, she told Linda, she had not focused on things that made her unhappy, since these were mercifully few and far between, but had instead concentrated on the ways in which she could improve her chances of happiness.

Inspired, Linda determined to do the same thing, and over the following week she analysed her life to determine where the gaps in her happiness were. Then she set about making a plan to fill the gaps.

Over the months that followed she found herself frequently being asked why she had a new-found spring in her step, and she was only too pleased to pass on the secret her colleague had told her.

HOW HAPPY ARE YOU – AND HOW ARE YOU HAPPY?

As the old expression maintains: 'There is more than one way to skin a cat.' This is certainly true for happiness, which can be experienced in a variety of ways, and to differing degrees, depending both on the situation and circumstances, and on the person involved. There a number of primary types of happiness, which can be broken down into ten headings:

- joy
- fulfilment
- contentment
- satisfaction
- pleasure
- excitement
- peace
- love
- accomplishment
- compassion.

This does not, of course, cover every possibility, and indeed that would be quite impossible since the list would be different for every reader, but it highlights the main areas in which, and through which, happiness can be experienced.

By having a clear understanding of these types of happiness, you can begin to identify which ones apply to you, and which do not. In other words, which of these sorts of happiness are you experiencing regularly in your life, and which are lacking? By knowing this, you can then identify how, where, why, and how frequently you experience each, allowing you to see which aspects of your life are bringing you happiness, and to see where the gaps are.

A useful exercise here is to list all the types of happiness and to map how they fit with your life. See which types of happiness you experience frequently and which less so, or not at all, and map them against your lifestyle to highlight the areas of your life that need to be improved in order to maximize your happiness. By seeing where there are significant omissions, and thereby seeing which areas of your life make you happy and which don't, you will be in a good position to begin to rectify the elements that could be improved.

Don't be surprised if the results are not as you might have anticipated; it is not uncommon for people to realize, for instance, that an area they thought wasn't working for them in fact brings them deep satisfaction – they simply hadn't thought of happiness in that way, while another area they believed made them really happy, in fact only does so in a limited way and can readily be improved.

HAPPY, HAPPIER, HAPPIEST

There are, of course, more than ten types of happiness, and myriad ways to be happy, and limiting yourself to just a few is a sure-fire way to limit your happiness. By experiencing as many as you can, you will experience happiness more often, in one of its many guises, and in doing so you will provide yourself with a fuller, more rounded happiness, one which is composed of a wide variety of sources, and not limited to one or two well-established routes.

If you realize that there are any types of happiness, or methods of experiencing them, of which you are not currently availing yourself, then finding ways of doing so, and engineering your lifestyle to accommodate them, is a quick and easy way to increase your happiness. By identifying as many possible types of happiness as you can that are relevant to you, and seeking as many sources for them as possible, you will automatically expand your repertoire for happiness, so it is well worth taking the time to really think it through, casting your net as wide as possible, and not simply assuming that you must already be experiencing happiness in all its forms, and on all available levels.

We have already looked at the ten primary sources of happiness for most people, but other forms of potential happiness that are worth exploring include:

- hedonism
- achievement
- anticipation
- altruism
- egoism
- selflessness
- charity
- self-fulfilment
- self-love
- self-worth.

Your list may include other types of happiness, or ways of experiencing it, too, and the more you can think of the better; just be sure that you don't simply list them but that you give yourself the best opportunity to actually experience them. Then review your list often, and enjoy the extra happiness it will bring you.

HAPPIER STILL

Defining the different types of happiness relevant to you, and the ways in which you can experience them, is a great starting-point, but it shouldn't be considered the complete solution. This is because every type of happiness is relevant to you, and if there are any that don't feature in your life at the moment, then you are missing a valuable opportunity for happiness.

Often, people don't realize that there are gaps in their happiness, or that they could be experiencing them much more often (or even that they are not doing so already), and sometimes people even feel that they don't deserve certain types of happiness, but the truth is that everyone deserves to be happy in every way — which, of course, includes making other people happy.

The key to maximizing your happiness lies in finding as many ways of being happy as you can, and in experiencing them as often as possible, and to the greatest possible degree. By spending as much of your time as you can being happy, and being really, really happy when you do so, you will elevate your life to a plane that is perfectly achievable — provided that you make your happiness a priority — but which most people never reach.

Putting it all together

By understanding the different things that make you happy, and the different ways in which you can be happy, you can ensure that you are experiencing the full spectrum of happiness as much of the time as possible.

Having a clear appreciation of the different ways in which happiness can manifest itself, as well as the different ways in which it can be created, and the different ways in which it can be experienced, you will be able to keep a constant watch on whether or not you are maximizing your happiness. If you are not (and the chances are that you are not), then you will need to identify those areas in which you are missing out, and plan a strategy to rectify the situation.

This can mean a lot of hard work initially, particularly if there are areas that do not feature at all in your life at the moment, but the amount of work required will lessen over time, while the benefits gained from the extra happiness you are able to enjoy will continue to grow and flourish.

29 The ten kinds of unhappy – and how to beat them

> 'Good humour is a tonic for mind and body. It is the best antidote for anxiety and depression. It is a business asset. It attracts and keeps friends. It lightens human burdens. It is the direct route to serenity and contentment.' Grenville Kleiser

> 'I had to learn compassion. Had to learn what it felt like to hate, and to forgive and to love and be loved. And to lose people close to me. Had to feel deep loneliness and sorrow. And then I could write.' Louise Penny

> 'I love the man that can smile in trouble, that can gather strength from distress, and grow brave by reflection. 'Tis the business of little minds to shrink, but he whose heart is firm, and whose conscience approves his conduct, will pursue his principles unto death.' Thomas Paine

> 'Every tomorrow has two handles. We can take hold of it with the handle of anxiety or the handle of faith.' Henry Ward Beecher

> 'We're taught to be ashamed of confusion, anger, fear and sadness, and to me they're of equal value to happiness, excitement and inspiration.' Alanis Morissette

The writer Franz Kafka, widely regarded as one of the most influential authors of the 20th-century, frequently wrote novels and short stories concerned with the themes of alienation, conflict and unhappiness. Indeed, in Kafka's first published book, *Betrachtung* (published in English as *Meditation* or *Contemplation*), a collection of 18 short stories written at the beginning of the 20th century, he includes one whose very title is 'Unhappiness'. It concerns the appearance of a child in the narrator's house, a presence that the narrator thinks may be a ghost, but he is unsure. In conversation with the child, he learns that they already know each other, and that the child is confused as to why the narrator is being so formal with him. As soon as he turns on a light, the child is gone, leading him to believe that the child was indeed a ghost. The child, it transpires, is part of the narrator's soul, trying to remind him of the child he once was, before he became alienated from the world, and from himself.

One of the many reasons for the popularity and enduring nature of Kafka's work, and for this type of story in particular, is that the theme of unhappiness is one to which we can all relate. Unhappiness affects everyone from time to time, even the most cheerful of people, and those who seem to enjoy all the good things in life. It is often unpredictable and can strike without warning; or it can be an ever-present menace, persistent and looming, until something is done to conquer it. It can come from many sources, and can adopt many guises, but to maximise your happiness you will need to minimise your unhappiness, and this will require that you keep a constant, vigilant watch for anything that might cause it, and that you act swiftly and robustly to counter it.

SO YOU THINK YOU'RE UNHAPPY?

Just as with happiness, unhappiness comes in a variety of guises. It can affect different people in different ways, but the one similarity is that any unhappiness, no matter how small, casts a negative shadow over your life, pulling you down, and needs to be remedied as quickly as possible in order to avoid it having a lasting negative impact. And just as you want to put in place first those things that will bring you the most happiness, so you will want to deal first with those areas of your life that are causing you the most unhappiness.

This is crucial, but it is often slow, hard work to complete, particularly where the unhappiness is longstanding, or set in a bedrock that will be hard to break down, such as depression or chronic anxiety. The techniques you will need to employ are much the same as those we have already looked at to highlight the areas of your life that are not bringing you as much happiness as they might.

First, you will need to identify which areas of your life are causing your unhappiness, being sure to make a note of how, when and why this is so, and the degree to which it is happening. Then you will need to think through how you can best remedy each situation. You will need to take each on its own merits, and devise an individual action plan for them all, since this is one area where a one-size-fits-all approach is unlikely to work. For each strategy you devise, make sure that you allocate a timeframe. This must be realistic, since trying to achieve too much, too soon, is unlikely to work, and any degree of failure may well hit you hard, making you even more unhappy. Finally, you will need to monitor the effectiveness of your solutions, taking the time to make adjustments as necessary. In this way, over time, you can be sure that the unhappiness in your life will be diminished, making way for you to maximize your happiness.

HOW MANY WAYS CAN YOU BE UNHAPPY?

Just as there are many ways to be happy, so there are also many ways to be unhappy. These include:

- despondency
- depression
- anxiety
- fear
- loneliness
- heartache
- bereavement
- loss other than bereavement (e.g. loss of opportunities, dreams, etc.)
- lack of fulfilment
- lack of self-worth.

It is perfectly possible that you might experience a combination of these, or other causes of unhappiness, and this can make the situation trickier to deal with. Unless the situation is dire, however, in which case you may well need to seek professional help, it can be remedied so that the unhappiness is minimized, or even eradicated. It is imperative that you isolate the cause, or causes, of any unhappiness you may experience, so that it can be dealt with effectively. If there are multiple causes, therefore, you will need to identify each in its own right, and build an action plan to remedy it devoted solely to that one area. Do this for as many areas as you need, but do not fall into the trap of trying to sort out several of them together.

CAN YOU EVER REALLY BE HAPPY?

Fortunately, although unhappiness is real, tangible and prevalent in our everyday lives, it need not be allowed to become central to them. Happiness and unhappiness are two sides of the same coin, and it is a coin that can be flipped to turn negative situations into positive ones. By identifying those areas of your life that are causing you unhappiness, and also identifying those areas that bring you joy, you can begin to map a route that best enables you to avoid the former while maximizing the latter. Even if your level of unhappiness is great, or the unhappiness you experience is acute, it can be remedied, and by working steadfastly towards your goal of maximizing your happiness, you can create a platform that enables you to be happy, at least most of the time.

Putting it all together

Unhappiness is unavoidable. It affects everyone at some times in their life, and the utopian dream of avoiding or eradicating unhappiness altogether is simply not realistic. It can, however, be minimized, and by identifying where and when in your life it is likely to strike, or if there are any areas that are making you continually unhappy, you can work to eliminate the sources of your unhappiness. This must be seen as an ongoing process, since different causes of unhappiness will occur at various times throughout your life. By getting into the habit of regularly reviewing your life with regards to any areas that are causing you unhappiness you will be certain not to allow any to take hold for very long, or even to establish themselves without you really noticing.

The eradication of unhappiness in your life, and the permanent presence of happiness, is your ultimate goal, and while it may not be quick or easy to implement, and will need constant review, it is possible to achieve. How quickly this can be accomplished will depend on how much time and effort you are willing to put into it, and also on your starting-point, but by never losing sight of the fact that anyone can enjoy a great deal of happiness, most of the time, you will be inspired to continue to work towards your goal – and what better goal can there possibly be than that of being happy?

(30) Money is everything

'Too many people spend money they haven't earned to buy things they don't want to impress people they don't like.'
Will Rogers

❝ 'If American men are obsessed with money, American women are obsessed with weight. The men talk of gain, the women talk of loss, and I do not know which talk is the more boring.'
Marya Mannes

❝ 'If money help a man to do good to others, it is of some value; but if not, it is simply a mass of evil, and the sooner it is got rid of, the better.' Swami Vivekananda

❝ 'Money is only a tool. It will take you wherever you wish, but it will not replace you as the driver.' Ayn Rand

❝ 'The lack of money is the root of all evil.' Mark Twain

Doug had everything. At least, he thought he did, until he met Mike. Doug had a lovely wife and two beautiful daughters, a good job, a large four-bedroomed house, a sports car, membership at a prestigious golf club – everything he could have wished for… until the day he met Mike in the club's bar. A chance encounter, but as the two men got chatting it became apparent that they had much in common, and soon they had struck up a good friendship. They agreed to meet once a week to play a round of golf, and all was going well until Mike invited Doug and his family to come to his house for a barbecue at the weekend.

Doug had been pleased to receive the invite, but when they arrived he discovered that Mike and his family lived in a seven-bedroom mansion. Flustered and perturbed, Doug quickly arranged a meeting with the bank manager, who agreed to arrange a new mortgage, and soon Doug and his family were settled into a seven-bedroom house neighbouring Mike's.

Then Doug noticed Mike's new car – a Ferrari. His previous car had been similar to Doug's, but this one changed the game completely. Using all their savings, and taking out a hefty loan, Doug purchased a Ferrari similar to Mike's. Then one day Mike suggested that Doug and his family might like to come and stay at Mike's weekend retreat, a large summerhouse in the mountains. Out of money and options, Doug felt defeated and despondent, and approached his wife apologetically with the bad news that they simply couldn't keep pace with Mike and his family any longer.

To his surprise, his wife seemed really happy, and Doug realized that he hadn't seen her this way for some while. She had, she informed him, become increasingly concerned at the way he was getting through their money, and also at the lack of time he was spending with her and with their children. Doug hadn't even noticed, but now he could see things for what they were, and he realized that he had been really unhappy ever since he tried to keep pace with Mike.

From now on, he decided, he would concentrate on what really mattered, and as to the money, he would just let the cards fall where they may.

WEALTH OR HAPPINESS?

It is easy to believe, with the trappings of modern life, that the more we have of everything – and especially money – the better off we'll be. Indeed, this is a message that is thrown at us from every conceivable direction, every day. It is at the centre of our culture where the desire, the need, to be winning the race to the big bucks and a large lifestyle is paramount.

More, faster, bigger, brighter, flashier – these, we are told, are what we should be striving for. But why? Will they improve our lot and make us happier? If that is truly the case then why is it that so many of the big money lottery winners wish they'd never won? Why isn't everyone who has 'made it' happy and relaxed? And how can so many poorer people from other cultures be so content?

The truth is that the pursuit of wealth and the pursuit of happiness are not the same thing, and the one won't necessarily lead to the other. Indeed, the endless exhausting chase can in itself lead to stress, discontent and ultimately misery. So perhaps it's time to take a step back. Perhaps it's time to re-evaluate the situation. Perhaps it's time to ask what we really want from life. If you had to choose, and could only have one or the other, which would you go for, money or happiness? It would have to be happiness, since money without happiness simply means you'll be richer being miserable, while being happy is the ultimate goal, however you get there.

So, while in an ideal world you perhaps wouldn't have to choose, in the real world you often do, so you need to be clear about your priorities.

SPENDING YOUR RESOURCES WISELY

Imagine completing a pie chart, dividing it according to where you currently spend your time and your energy; then completing another apportioning the space according to those things that you most enjoy, which are most fulfilling and which give you energy. If the two don't tally then you are not spending your time and energy in the most important and appropriate areas. Worse, you are spending them on things that may be actively sapping your energy and your morale. And unless you find the time to stop to re-evaluate the situation, and the space in which to step back and see the bigger picture, the true picture, then you will in all probability continue spinning aimlessly on life's hamster wheel with no chance of redirection.

So what is it that really makes you happy? What, in your life as it currently is, really brings you joy, or fulfilment, or pride, or any of the other ways in which you can be happy, and what else would do so but is currently missing?

Look at your second chart and see just how much time you're spending in ways that can make you happy, and how much time you're allocating to pursuits that can't. Then find ways to spend more time on the former and less time on the latter. It sounds easy, but of course there are plenty of things in everyone's life that they would change in a heartbeat if they could, but which cannot reasonably be altered. Yet that still leaves lots of things which can, and it's these on which you need to focus, starting with the lowest-hanging fruit and gradually working your way upwards. It really is worth putting in the time and effort to get this aspect of your life working as well for you as it can, and remember that although it may take some time to complete, you will begin to reap the rewards of your first changes almost straight away.

FAILURE AND INADEQUACY

For many people, not having enough money leads to feelings of inadequacy and even failure. Far too often, however, what constitutes 'enough' in this context is not governed by how much money they need, nor even by how much they want, but by how much other people expect them to have, or the financial position they perceive others to consider them to be in. This is, of course, a recipe for disaster since other people's expectations of us are seldom likely to be lower than the real situation, and also seldom likely to be realistic.

When you find yourself in this situation (and it is more likely to be 'when' rather than 'if'), there are three courses of action you can take:

- Earn more money to increase your income.
- Spend less money to decrease your outgoings.
- Reframe your position.

For many people, the first of these is not an option, or at least not one that can be triggered any time soon. And the second course of action is fine if you want to reallocate your funds, provided that you can find ways to cut back, but it won't help with your overall financial situation. Which leaves the third, and most viable option. Reframing your position is the best, and longest-lasting solution, since it is the only one that deals with the core issues, which is to say other people's opinion of you, and the way that makes you feel about yourself, and your opinion of yourself, as governed by your wealth and possessions.

Your happiness will take a major hit if you spend your life trying to 'keep up with the Joneses', since there will always be people with more money than you, and so you can never really win, and never being satisfied with what you have but always striving to get the next, bigger, shinier thing will do the same. Think about it – no matter how big a house you get you can always get bigger, and if you always want more you will always be disappointed. Maybe your house doesn't have a conservatory and you really want one. You work hard and save up and get one but then your attention turns to wanting a bigger house, a swimming-pool, a self-contained annexe, grounds, helicopter pad, golf course, better golf course, etc.

At what point along this seemingly endless quest will you be happy? And what if, like the vast majority of people, you never get there? You are setting yourself up to be disillusioned and disappointed, and maybe even to feel like a failure – no matter how well you're doing. So the only sensible solution is to address the problem by reframing your position.

If you already have a home, then you're doing well and should be pleased, even if it doesn't have any of the other things. And you should ensure that you enjoy it for what it is, not waste time fretting over what it's not. In all probability, when it comes to money and possessions you are doing well, compared to the majority of people in the world, so make the decision to enjoy what you have, and to stop ceaselessly chasing more and feeling disappointed.

Putting it all together

Judging yourself by how much money you have, and what material possessions you earn, is very likely to cause you unhappiness since there is no end point to what you could achieve, and so it is difficult to ever feel successful – and happy with what you have. Even worse is allowing other people to influence you by worrying about how much money they have, or what they must think of you and your house, car, holidays, etc. The only thing that matters in the quest to be happy is that you have enough to enjoy, not that you could have even more.

Money certainly isn't everything, and some of the poorest people are some of the happiest; besides, judging your happiness by how much money you have is a very narrow way of viewing the world — it is far better to judge your happiness by how happy you are! You will never have 100 per cent of the money in the world, and you may never have 100 per cent of the things on your bucket list, but you can be 100 per cent happy, and that is what really counts.

31 Write your own obituary

> 'All our dreams can come true, if we have the courage to pursue them.' Walt Disney

> 'Every great dream begins with a dreamer. Always remember, you have within you the strength, the patience and the passion to reach for the stars to change the world.' Harriet Tubman

> 'Without leaps of imagination, or dreaming, we lose the excitement of possibilities. Dreaming, after all, is a form of planning.' Gloria Steinem

> 'To accomplish great things, we must not only act, but also dream; not only plan, but also believe.' Anatole France

> 'First comes thought; then organization of that thought, into ideas and plans; then transformation of those plans into reality. The beginning, as you will observe, is in your imagination.' Napoleon Hill

In 1985 an Australian businessman named Geoffrey decided that his life had become boring, and that, at the age of 44, he hadn't achieved anywhere near as much as he had thought he would have done by that age. His lack of success bothered him, but the chief reason for his malaise was that he couldn't see how things would ever change. He pictured the future, and the future he pictured did not look rosy, at least not to him, though many people would have been quite happy with it. Determined to take action to rectify the situation, and to secure his happiness for the future, Geoffrey wrote out his own obituary, detailing everything as he hoped it would be, years into the future. Then he set about putting it into action.

The first thing he did was to leave his job at a large insurance company in Melbourne, and head out into the Outback, where he took a job at an ore-processing plant in order to learn as much as he could about the industry. He loved it, and with renewed enthusiasm he set about launching his own company. To begin with it was just him, then person by person he was able to expand, until after two years he was employing eight workers. He invested the company's profits in exploration, and two years later they were rewarded when they found, and claimed, an untapped seam of copper worth millions of dollars. Rather than simply sell it on to one of the larger companies, Geoffrey decided to take the long way round, and had his company carry out the work.

It took them 14 years, by which time the company had more than 400 employees and Geoffrey was an extremely wealthy man indeed. He then decided to sell the firm he had started, and retire to a lavish property on Sydney's famous waterfront. And the most remarkable thing? This was exactly what he had pictured for himself, at this point in his life, when he wrote his obituary all those years before.

SEE INTO THE FUTURE

Writing your own obituary may sound like a bizarre exercise (and rather morbid to boot!), but the reason for it is simple – by envisioning your future, and describing it exactly as you hope it will be, you have a clear and defined target to work towards, one that will bring you happiness every time you think of it and inspire you to work towards your dream.

It is a self-actualizing exercise, so try to describe it in as much detail as possible. Where will you be? What will you be doing? What will you have achieved by then? And so on. How realistic you decide to keep it depends very much on what works best for you, but a general rule of thumb is to create a vision that is ambitious, but not completely unrealistic.

A well-thought-out and pragmatic vision can form a point of reference for you for the future, a control chart against which you can map your progress; so if your targets are beyond the bounds of what might reasonably be achieved with a lot of hard work and a pinch of good fortune, then their worth is dramatically diminished. Worse, you may be simply setting yourself up for a fall.

CONSIDER THE PRESENT AND CHART YOUR POSITION

Next, you need to plot your current position. Below are some of the elements you might wish to consider:

- What is your current job?
- Where do you live?
- What is your family situation?
- What hobbies do you pursue?
- What key factors, if any, are missing from your life?

Honesty is key here, and remember that the list need be for your eyes only. If you pretend that you are much closer to achieving your dream than you really are, then you are likely to be disappointed as time goes by that you don't seem to be making any progress, or even that you appear to have slipped back.

Equally important, however, is to resist the temptation to pretend that you have achieved less than you really have, just so that further down the track, when you revisit this exercise, you can convince yourself that you are doing better than you really are!

A true and accurate picture of your real position at present may not make great reading straight after you have envisaged the future, but that's fine – the whole point of this exercise is to determine the steps necessary in order to turn that vision into reality.

PLOT YOUR COURSE TO ATTAIN YOUR DREAM

Next, you need to plot the points in between these two ends of the spectrum, to see how you can realistically work towards achieving your dream.

- Are you happy in your current job but want to progress, or do you need to change careers in order to fulfil your dreams? What do you need to do to make this happen?
- Are you living where you want to be living, and in your preferred type of accommodation? If not, what changes do you need to make in order to be able to move?
- What is it that you want to achieve in life? What step-ping-stones need to be put in place in order to make this happen?

And so on. Then, you simply need to join the dots. You know where you are at the moment. You know where you want to be. You know the requisite steps along the way so you know how you will achieve it. You know what assistance you will require and from whom, and you know the timescale for each. So you have everything you need to plot your maximum growth potential for happiness, and every reason to believe you can get it there.

Whether you choose to share your dreams with anyone else, or to keep them strictly private, is entirely up to you, but your decision should be based on which is likely to make you happiest. If broadcasting your aspirations is likely just to make you more anxious, since other people will be able to watch to see whether or not you achieve them, then it is best to keep your cards close to your chest.

Putting it all together

Writing your own obituary is a great way of seeing what the future might hold for you if you follow the course you are currently on; where ideally you would like to end up; and what you will need to change in your life in order to reach your preferred destination. Your happiness will be greatly affected by the path you choose to follow, and whether or not this will ultimately lead to you achieving your goals; so use this exercise both as a reality check, and as a great way of inspiring you to follow your dreams.

Remember that it is only as useful as it is accurate, so try to revisit it now and then to refresh it, and keep it up to date. As odd as it may sound, by always having at the back of your mind what you will have achieved by the time you die, you can usefully measure your current happiness, and also gain a valuable insight into how happy you are likely to be in the future. And by seeing what you need to change in order to increase your potential for happiness, you can get a head start on working to provide it.

32 Peace, tranquillity and calm... Now! Now! Now!

❝ *'It is neither wealth nor splendour; but tranquillity and occupation which give you happiness.'* Thomas Jefferson

❝ *'Success and failure are emotional and physiological experiences. We need to deal with them in a way that is present and calm.'* Chade-Meng Tan

❝ *'I've worked with people at different stages of their careers and different success levels, and one thing I've noticed about the guys at the top is they're so relaxed and calm – it's about not having anything to prove except doing good work.'* Shawn Roberts

❝ *'Periods of tranquillity are seldom prolific of creative achievement. Mankind has to be stirred up.'* Alfred North Whitehead

❝ *'It is in vain to say human beings ought to be satisfied with tranquillity: they must have action; and they will make it if they cannot find it.'* Charlotte Brontë

A man who lived in a coastal village would take some exercise every morning by running along the beach, and then going for a swim in the sea. One evening, threatening storm clouds began to gather, darkening the sky, and before long it had begun to rain, and the wind had started to gather its strength, until it rattled the windows and shook the doors. The rain became heavier, and the storm built and built in intensity and ferocity, until it became a storm such as the man had never seen before. In the morning, the man awoke to bright blue skies, and a gentle breeze, and since the storm appeared to have blown itself out he decided to go for his run as usual.

He ran through the glistening streets, and on down towards the beach, but as he approached he noticed that the sand seemed to be an unusual colour. Where normally it was a pale yellow, it was now pinkish, and instead of being a uniform shade it now appeared to be flecked. As he drew nearer, the scene before him became more distinct, and when he reached the edge of the sand he simply stood there, transfixed by what lay before him, for the sand was now littered with millions of pale pink starfish. The freak storm had evidently played tricks with the sea, and somehow caused it to wash ashore all these tiny creatures which, the man knew, would not survive long out of the water, particularly when the sun rose above the cliffs and spilled on to the beach.

Quickly, he made up his mind and, careful to avoid stepping on any of the starfish, he walked onto the beach and down to the water's edge. When he got there he reached down and picked up one of the little fish, and threw it gently back into the water. Then he did the same for another, and another, and another, until he ached from the effort, but still he kept on going. Another man saw what he was doing and said: 'My friend, there must be millions of starfish washed ashore on this stretch of beach alone. Do you really think that what you're doing will make a difference?' The man paused for a moment to consider his answer, then he reached down and picked up another starfish. 'It will for this one,' he said, and threw it back into the sea.

FIND PERSONAL PEACE

It is difficult to experience happiness when you are feeling stressed, anxious, worried, frantic, angry or any of the many other ways that can shatter your calm. Indeed, peace is becoming increasingly elusive in the modern world, with all manner of things able to disrupt it. And yet experiencing peace, calm and tranquillity, at least occasionally, is essential for your long-term wellbeing and happiness. One of the reasons that this fundamental need is so often overlooked is that it is far too easy not to notice its omission.

Packing your life with things that keep you busy is often seen as positive, and the tendency is for people to try to fit in more and more. The thought behind this is simple – the more you do, the more you will experience, and the more chances you will have of being successful, whatever your goals. This is all well and good, provided that you allow room for peace and calm too, and this means making space for them in your life. This, of course, necessarily means that there will have to be times when you do very little, but this is fine – indeed, it is the whole point. Only in sustained periods of downtime can you truly experience the calming effect of peace, and it is in doing so that you strengthen the foundations on which you build everything else in your life, including happiness. So it is crucial that you create the necessary space to enjoy the peace, tranquillity and calm that is always available, but which is so often ignored. Whenever possible, try to allow a decent amount of time for it, but remember that even just a few minutes can make a real difference, and that the benefit from these will accumulate over time. If you can allow two or three hours at a time, though, at least once a month, you will soon begin to reap the rewards by finding a personal peace which in turn can lead to profound happiness.

YOUR MENTAL SPA

If the idea of allowing sufficient time away from everything, in order to benefit from the tranquillity this allows, seems to you to be an alien concept, then try looking at it this way: happiness is an emotion, something that you feel, but something which also stems from your thoughts and experiences. The same is true of unhappiness, and in the quest to maximize the former and minimize the latter, you will need to allow yourself sufficient space to properly organize your thoughts, and your feelings. In the same way that visiting a spa provides total relaxation for your body, allowing it to recover from the stresses under which it is placed every day, and to rejuvenate, so the same is true of creating for yourself the time and space to completely relax your mind. This is your 'mental spa', a place to where you can retreat, whenever you need, to allow your mind to escape the daily stresses under which it is placed, and to rejuvenate. In this way you are freeing your mind of all the clutter that would otherwise impede it, and clearing the way to experience happiness with renewed vigour and vitality.

RETREAT, RETREAT, RETREAT!

One of the best ways to experience complete tranquillity and calm is to go on a retreat. The idea of these is simple – for a short period of time, usually a weekend or a week (but they can be just for a day), you go somewhere that is devoted to taking you away from the hectic rush of everyday life and simplifying things so that, devoid of distractions and interruptions, you can concentrate on finding real and lasting peace. It is amazing what a difference it makes to have all the technology on which we come to rely removed. With no Internet access, no telephones, no tablets or computers, and often not even any television or radio, your mind is given the space it needs to relax and become calm. Doing this allows you to take a mental step back from your everyday life, so that you can see where the gaps are, and where you are doing too much. It affords you a wonderful opportunity to take stock of your situation, and to see which elements of your life are really providing you with happiness, and where happiness is being kept at bay by things simply getting in the way. It also gives you the chance to prioritize the things in your life, and to decide whether or not you are properly nourishing those things which will bring you the most happiness.

Putting it all together

Freeing yourself to experience real peace is one of the simplest yet most rewarding things you can do in the quest for happiness. It is, however, one of the areas that is most often neglected. With the right approach, though, it can be a quick and easy way to boost your happiness frequently. Even short periods of downtime, away from the strains and stresses of everyday life, can be really beneficial, and these can be experienced anywhere and at any time.

Try to get into the habit of seizing every opportunity you can to relax your mind, and the more you practise the quicker you will be able to reach a state of blissful neutrality. If possible, try to find a few hours every now and then when you can tune out and just relax. By having a sustained period like this you will be able to relax more fully, finding a peace and calm that can have far-reaching benefits to your happiness. If you're too busy in life, then you might just be too busy to be happy, so prioritize peace, calm and tranquillity in your life, and enjoy the rewards they bring.

33 Make as many mistakes as you can

❝ 'A life spent making mistakes is not only more honourable, but more useful than a life spent doing nothing.' George Bernard Shaw

❝ 'A man must be big enough to admit his mistakes, smart enough to profit from them, and strong enough to correct them.' John C. Maxwell

❝ 'Most people die of a sort of creeping common sense, and discover when it is too late that the only things one never regrets are one's mistakes.' Oscar Wilde

❝ 'You build on failure. You use it as a stepping stone. Close the door on the past. You don't try to forget the mistakes, but you don't dwell on it. You don't let it have any of your energy, or any of your time, or any of your space.' Johnny Cash

❝ 'Some of the worst mistakes of my life have been haircuts.' Jim Morrison

The airline industry faced a growing problem in the form of bird strikes, where birds that flew into, or were struck by, aircraft could seriously damage the cockpit glass. In light of this, a research company developed a new, prototype safety glass, specifically designed to withstand such impacts. In order to demonstrate its efficacy, the research company invited representatives from companies throughout the industry to attend a demonstration of its new product. In order to make it as memorable as possible, they had borrowed a jumbo jet, fitted it with their new glass, and arranged to have a chicken fired at it from a cannon; after all, if it could withstand a chicken propelled at it at the same speed at which the planes flew, then the glass could certainly withstand the impact of the smaller birds which were the usual culprits. To give it an added flourish, and to reassure the audience of their faith in the product, the chairman of the research company had decided to sit in the cockpit when the cannon was fired.

When the moment arrived, and as the gathered spectators looked on with interest, the signal was given and the cannon was duly fired. To a blast of smoke and a deafening roar, the chicken shot out of the cannon, across the hangar, and smashed straight through the glass, narrowly missing the startled chairman, and continued to smash its way through a sizeable portion of the aircraft, before coming to an abrupt stop as it wedged itself somewhere towards the rear of the aeroplane.

When the dust had settled, literally and figuratively, and a post mortem was carried out to establish just what had gone wrong, it transpired that the new safety glass was, in fact, entirely strong enough for the job, and the cannon had acted exactly as intended. The only problem had been a misunderstanding by the cannon's operator in sourcing the poultry. Not given explicit instructions, it hadn't occurred to him to purchase a fresh bird, and he had in fact fired a frozen chicken at the aircraft.

Fortunately, no one was hurt, and the demonstration had certainly been memorable, plus the people involved had learned valuable lessons. So all in all the event could be regarded as a success.

BE PREPARED TO ALWAYS LEARN FROM YOUR MISTAKES

If you can learn to learn from your mistakes, then it stands to reason that the more mistakes you make, the more you will be able to learn. And by learning in this way you will grow as a person, and in a very personal way, since the mistakes you make are your own, so the experience will necessarily be tailored to you.

People who are willing to take risks, knowing that they run the risk of making mistakes along the way, give themselves the opportunity to develop in a way that those who seek only the safe options do not; and the more that you attempt to accomplish in your life, and the more risks that you are willing to take, the more mistakes you will make – and thus the more opportunities for growth you will have afforded yourself. So never be afraid of making mistakes, since each error will merely present you with an opportunity for learning and development, and by taking this approach, instead of shying away from taking opportunities that arise, particularly if their outcome seems uncertain, you will give yourself the best chance to benefit from your experiences.

DON'T WASTE TIME DWELLING ON YOUR MISTAKES

Making mistakes is a good thing, but dwelling on them is not. Since mistakes are, by definition, things that have gone wrong, dwelling on them will only make you spend an unhealthy amount of time mulling over negative experiences. Instead, what you need to do in order to gain the most from the opportunities you have, and to make yourself happy as a consequence, is to learn the lessons from your mistakes quickly, and then cut away from the thoughts, clinically and terminally.

The key is not to keep remembering what went wrong, but to remember the lesson that you drew from the experience. Constantly reminding yourself of the time that you were late, with disastrous consequences, and going over and over in your head all the reasons why this happened, is unlikely to be productive – rather, it is likely to make you depressed and quickly give you a headache!

Remembering instead that the lesson was to make sure that you arrive early to appointments, and that in order to do that you need to learn not to always try to squeeze in one more thing before you go (which inevitably makes you late), and acting on it so that you are happier as a result of the actions that your mistake led to, is a positive outcome, and one that will serve you well, in a positive manner.

LEARN FROM THE MISTAKES THAT OTHERS HAVE MADE

If making mistakes of your own is a positive thing due to the opportunity for learning and improvement that they offer you, then the same can be said of learning from the mistakes of others. In fact, this can be even better since, if you get it right, you can reap the rewards without having to go through the process of making the mistake in the first place! It doesn't matter how many mistakes you make so long as you never make the same one twice – which, of course, you won't provided that you have learned the available lessons from them. And if you add to your mistakes the mistakes of others, you can increase the opportunities for growth without too much extra effort.

Better still, other people may make mistakes that you never would, since they may be in situations you would never encounter, or simply because they handle things in a very different way, so by capitalizing on their errors you can improve your ability to avoid mistakes in the future, and at the same time broaden your horizons.

Keep a weather eye out for mistakes of all kinds, in any and every situation, and learn from them so that you don't have to make the same mistakes.

Putting it all together

Properly handled, making mistakes can be a great way of improving your happiness. By learning from them, and drawing out lessons that will enable you to do things in an improved manner in the future, you will enable yourself to go about your business with a much better chance of being happy as a result.

Learning the available lessons from your mistakes, or those of others, may help you in the future to be more efficient, more productive, more focused, more generous, or a host of other attributes, each of which will contribute to your ability to be happy. It is important to remember that the quicker you can learn the lessons, and the more clinical you can be in your execution of this, the more cheerful you will remain, since you will not be allowing yourself to dwell on negative thoughts, nor to wallow in self-pity.

Examine what happened, what went wrong and why, and quickly decide how you could have done things better, and what adjustments you need to make for the next time. Then move on. By getting past this point quickly, not only will you ensure that your mistakes do not assume a disproportionately large degree of importance for you, but also that you can begin to capitalize as soon as possible on the benefits the lessons you have learned will give you.

(34) Move to a happier place

> **"** 'Human beings are the only animal that thinks they change who they are simply by moving to a different place. Birds migrate, but it's not quite the same thing.' Douglas Coupland

> **"** 'The great thing in the world is not so much where we stand, as in what direction we are moving.' Oliver Wendell Holmes, Sr

> **"** 'Common sense and a sense of humour are the same thing, moving at different speeds. A sense of humour is just common sense, dancing.' William James

> **"** 'I tell you the past is a bucket of ashes, so live not in your yesterdays, not just for tomorrow, but in the here and now. Keep moving and forget the post mortems; and remember, no one can get the jump on the future.' Carl Sandburg

> **"** 'You have to come to your closed doors before you get to your open doors… What if you knew you had to go through 32 closed doors before you got to your open door? Well, then you'd come to closed door number eight and you'd think, "Great, I got another one out of the way"… Keep moving forward.' Joel Osteen

In 1967 a Canadian multi-millionaire visited a remote part of India with a view to opening a factory in the region, in order to benefit from the comparatively inexpensive workforce. During his visit he met many of the villagers whose lives would be radically altered, and he took the opportunity to tell them how much better off they would be once his factory began its operation. They listened carefully to everything he had to say, and weighed it all up with open minds, but to his great surprise and disappointment they said that they would not want to work at the factory. The reason, they said, was simply that they enjoyed their lives the way they were. The millionaire found this incredible. These people lived in slums, they had barely enough food to eat nor sufficient clothing to satisfy their needs, and yet here they were turning down his offer for improvement. He put this to them, and their reply was to change his life forever.

They told him that while they could see the attraction in many of the benefits the lifestyle he was offering would afford them, they also believed that working at his factory would be detrimental to their happiness. They would have money, but they would also have stress. They would have new clothes, but they would have new worries. Their future employment would be guaranteed, but not their future happiness. All this, they told him, was in stark contrast to their current position, where they lacked the amenities he was describing but where they were consistently truly and deeply happy. And wasn't this, after all, the main thing, they asked him? He considered their answer for a moment, and realized that they were right. All the benefits that he was offering them would not be benefits at all if they did not improve the lives of the recipients, and if they felt that they already had everything they needed, and indeed wanted, then his factory could only serve to do them harm. So he reversed his decision to locate a factory in the village, and on returning to Canada he sold the majority of his possessions, as well as his company, and moved to India where he lived a more frugal existence, but one which was undoubtedly happier.

LEARN FROM OTHER COUNTRIES

The Kingdom of Bhutan, a tiny landlocked country located at the eastern end of the Himalayas, is home to approximately 750,000 people, the majority of whom do not earn enough money to have to pay tax, and is lacking in most of the infrastructure that is taken for granted in 'first world' countries. Yet a 2006 *Business*

Week global survey rated Bhutan as the happiest country in Asia, and the eighth happiest place in the world. So what makes this tiny kingdom, poor by global standards, such a great place to live?

There are a number of theories, but most of them agree that the country's residents enjoy happy lives since they have everything they need, and their needs and wants are relatively simple. Simply put, most of Bhutan's population does not crave a millionaire lifestyle, but instead enjoys simpler pleasures, but pleasures which are attainable, and which they are therefore able to enjoy frequently, and to the full. In this way, although their lives might, to outsiders, seem simple, they are in fact deeply fulfilling, and by having everything they need and everything they want, they maintain a level of happiness that is the envy of virtually every other nation. Indeed, it may well be the complexity of modern living in developed countries, and the sheer, baffling array of commodities, amusements, possessions, opportunities, luxuries, and even what we have come to think of as necessities, which causes much of the unhappiness we sometimes feel. Life has become so complicated in countries where even something as simple as selecting a loaf of bread to purchase presents the consumer with so many options it can become a stressful experience, that two unwanted things happen:

- Even simple tasks, or tasks that should be pleasurable, can become anxiety-provoking, negative experiences.
- So much time is taken up with sorting out the mundane, everyday tasks, that we have less time available to spend in the pursuit of activities that make us happy.

By following the example set by Bhutan and its residents, we can simplify our lives and in so doing eliminate much of the unnecessary stress and anxiety to which we so readily (and often unwittingly) subject ourselves every day; we can also learn to stop reaching for the impossible and improbable, and instead enjoy to the full all the things that we already have.

BROADEN YOUR HORIZONS

It stands to reason that the more things you learn to appreciate, the greater the number of potential opportunities for happiness you will have. Take as an example, sport. If you only enjoy watching tennis, then your opportunities to gain pleasure from watching sport will be limited. If you can learn to appreciate, and even enjoy, a wider range of sports, perhaps adding football, athletics and snooker to your sporting repertoire, then your opportunities for experiencing the happiness such viewing brings will be greatly increased. Furthermore, you might decide to take up one of these sports, maybe even join a team and compete in a league, further increasing your potential opportunities for enjoyment. And the sports you watch can be enjoyed even more by deepening your knowledge of them; maybe you even go and watch them live, sometimes, instead of just on the television.

And that's just looking at one small area of your life. By taking this approach to your whole life, not just to your hobbies and interests but your work, family and commitments you may have, etc., you can quickly expand the opportunities for happiness with which you are presented. So try to develop a broad range of interests and actively pursue them, and try to maximize the enjoyment that can be gained from each.

MENTAL MOVING

While Bhutan may be one of the happiest places on Earth, and therefore ostensibly a great place to live if you want to be happy, the practicalities of actually upping sticks and moving there may well bring about more negatives than positives for you! So perhaps actually physically moving your life, lock, stock and barrel, to a happier place is impractical and self-defeating, but there is another, simpler, way to gain many of the benefits of moving there, without the inconvenience. By adopting the approach of the Bhutanese people, and trying to derive the maximum enjoyment that we can from life's simpler pleasures, as well as by simplifying our lives wherever possible, we can take a leaf out of their book and begin to experience many of the benefits they enjoy, without significantly compromising our own lives.

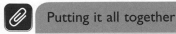

Putting it all together

Moving to another country, one that is ostensibly happier than our own, is probably not the most sensible answer for most of us. However, it is perfectly possible – and practical – to derive many of the benefits they enjoy without having to emigrate! By learning from their outlook, and their approach to life, and by adopting some of their fundamental principles outright, and by adapting others to suit our needs, we can alter elements of our lives to allow us to derive more enjoyment from our everyday living. We can also broaden our horizons, and develop a wider range of interests to pursue, in order to enable us to derive enjoyment from more things, more often.

Simplification is one of the key learnings from countries like Bhutan, where the pursuit of the extraordinary and lavish is ignored, in favour of enjoying what is actually there to enjoy. Although we may dream of winning lots of money, and crave many of the possessions and experiences which we imagine that would bring us, if we can instead learn to focus on enjoying those things we actually have, here and now, we can experience immediate and tangible happiness, rather than simply dreaming of things that might make us happier – even though the reality might be quite different.

35 The happiness gym

> ❝ 'Research has shown that the best way to be happy is to make each day happy.' Deepak Chopra

> ❝ 'I am determined to be cheerful and happy in whatever situation I may find myself. For I have learned that the greater part of our misery or unhappiness is determined not by our circumstance but by our disposition.' Martha Washington

> ❝ 'To be wholly devoted to some intellectual exercise is to have succeeded in life.' Robert Louis Stevenson

> ❝ 'Be happy with what you have and are, be generous with both, and you won't have to hunt for happiness.' William E. Gladstone

> ❝ 'He who enjoys doing and enjoys what he has done is happy.' Johann Wolfgang von Goethe

In the 1950s the Royal Canadian Air Force, concerned that a number of its personnel were becoming unfit, devised a revolutionary new fitness programme. Unlike others of its day, it did not centre around which was better for you, a cardiovascular workout or strengthening exercises, but instead used as its basis the people who would be using it, and in particular the limitations of the specific situations.

Those who were becoming unfit by and large fell into two categories – they were either desk-bound, or they were pilots or navigators.

The two key elements that were leading to their loss of fitness were determined as lack of time and the confines of their workspace. In other words, the people developing the programme had not taken the approach of 'exercise takes time, and you need a large space to do it properly', but had instead tailored the exercises to the limitations of those who would be using them. The result was brilliant – a full workout that could be completed in just 15 minutes, which could be performed while sitting at a desk or in a cockpit, and which required no specialist equipment.

As a result, it worked. It was manageable, people had no excuse for not doing it, and so they did it. And while the results took a while to show, they were significant and long-lasting – and the benefits could be enjoyed from day one.

The same is true of your happiness. In order to maximize your mental wellbeing you will need to invest the necessary time and effort to strengthen and tone your 'mental muscles'. Just as for the Royal Canadian Air Force's exercise routine, your happiness programme need not take any longer than 10-15 minutes per day, and can be completed anywhere, without the need for specialist equipment! And just as with the exercise programme, you really have no excuse not to do it...

ENSURE YOU TAKE REGULAR HAPPINESS EXERCISE

Because happiness is a somewhat abstract concept, it is easy to dismiss the need to work at it, but doing so comes at a price. Also, it is simply not logical. If you want to get physically fitter, you wouldn't just expect it to happen, with no thought or effort on your part, would you? You would exercise, investing the time and effort required to get results, and this seems entirely sensible. In the same way, if you want to lose weight you might exercise and also reduce your calorie intake. Why then, if you want to improve your happiness, would you not take the same approach? Think of it as a form of exercise – after all, that's what it is, it just happens to be mental rather than physical. Imagine that your happiness is not an emotional but a physical entity. If you want to strengthen it you will need to exercise the relevant parts. And doing so only every now and then is insufficient – you will need to commit to a programme of exercise and stick to it.

PREPARE TO STRENGTHEN YOUR HAPPINESS MUSCLES

A regular workout for your body strengthens the muscles, allowing you, over time, to be able to do more, with less effort. It also gives you a mental lift; and even just using your muscles each day in the normal course of events helps to keep them toned and ready for action.

So it is with your happiness. By taking the time to actually work on your happiness, by using the various exercises and techniques described in this book, you will strengthen your happiness, in several ways:

- You will constantly push your maximum happiness level, and also your happiness endurance, allowing you to be happier, for longer.
- You will find it easier to reach your maximum happiness, and quicker to do so.
- You will develop reserves of happiness, which will be ready and waiting for you when you need them.

Remember, too, that you can keep your happiness toned simply by using it frequently. In other words, by being constantly aware of the opportunities for happiness that occur every day, but which we so often overlook or simply don't notice, you will keep your ability to be happy primed and ready.

Think of it this way – imagine a morose person, someone who does not employ each opportunity to be happy. When such opportunities arise, how ready will they be to take them? How quickly will they be able to take advantage of them? Will it be a reflex action, or something they really have to try hard to achieve? And what will be their maximum potential for happiness? Then imagine the opposite of all this – happiness nirvana – a state that can be achieved by anyone who is willing to work at it.

HAPPINESS AEROBICS

In the same way as working to strengthen your happiness will allow you to reach a higher degree of happiness, working to improve your happiness stamina and flexibility will allow you to enjoy being happy on more occasions, and to maintain that happiness for longer. It's the equivalent of spending time on the treadmill at the gym, or going for long walks. With either of these, the secret would be to do them for a sustained period, perhaps an hour or so at a time, and to do them regularly, three or four times a week. After all, you wouldn't expect to see noticeable improvements in your stamina without putting in regular effort, would you? So it is with improving your happiness stamina. You will need to be aware of every opportunity to exercise your happiness, and then find ways of maintaining it for as long as possible.

Over time, this will become easier, and begin to happen naturally, requiring less effort on your part. And the more often you do it, the quicker you will begin to see the results, and to enjoy the benefits.

Putting it all together

Happiness is naturally occurring and with the right approach it can be found in all manner of places without too much effort on your part, but its frequency, strength and duration can all be improved through working at it with regular exercise.

Just as with physical fitness, the starting point will vary from person to person, and so will the maximum potential that can be reached, but it is only by taking regular exercise for happiness, and working to improve your happiness fitness level, that you will be able to reach your full potential. And just as with physical exercise, the more you put in, the more you will get out.

The best approach is to not simply leave it to chance to find opportunities to work on your happiness, but to schedule them. Try to find a set time each day, or even each week, when you can look back at the opportunities for happiness that presented themselves, and decide whether or not you made the most of them — and if not, why not. What could you have done better? What should you do next time in a similar situation? And so on. Equally, were there any opportunities that you bypassed? Or was there anything that you did, or failed to do, which prevented you from taking advantage of an opportunity for happiness?

By investing in these exercises to improve your happiness and spending the time to work through your situation in this way, you will, over time, improve your ability to seize the opportunities as they occur, and even to create them.

Keep things in perspective

> 'I believe everyone should have a broad picture of how the universe operates and our place in it. It is a basic human desire. And it also puts our worries in perspective.' Stephen Hawking

> 'Everything we hear is an opinion, not a fact. Everything we see is a perspective, not the truth.' Marcus Aurelius

> 'Winners have the ability to step back from the canvas of their lives like an artist gaining perspective. They make their lives a work of art — an individual masterpiece.' Denis Waitley

> 'A brain haemorrhage puts it all in a deeper perspective. I'm one of those guys hit by lightning. I see the big picture. Everything is in perspective now. Let's just say I'm the kind of guy who knows how to enjoy the moment.' Bret Michaels

> 'When you wake up every day, you have two choices. You can either be positive or negative; an optimist or a pessimist. I choose to be an optimist. It's all a matter of perspective.'
> Harvey Mackay

A man decided that what he really wanted out of life was to be happy. A noble thought, and one to which most people would ascribe, but one which most of us spend very little time actively pursuing, or even thinking about how we might achieve it. So he conscientiously set about thinking what it was he needed to do in order to realize his aim. When he had thought it through he compiled a list, and put all the items in order of priority. Somewhere near the top was 'learning to drive'. This seemed a sensible place to start since he could get it underway almost immediately, and three months later he passed his test, at the second time of asking. He had achieved his goal, and given himself a reason to be happy. But it didn't. Instead, it really bothered him that he hadn't passed first time. He knew there could be any number of reasons – having a bad day, being paired with a particularly harsh examiner, simple bad luck, and so on – but it niggled so much that he decided the only way to put his mind at rest was to take the advanced driving test. After months of preparation he passed first time, and got a number of 1s on his test sheet, and nothing lower than 2. But again, instead of being delighted with his achievement, he fixated on the fact that he hadn't got a perfect score. Then, at last, it dawned on him that the only reason for doing any of this was to make himself happier, and he realized that this would never happen unless he could alter his outlook on life, and learn to be a little gentler on himself. Above all, he needed to learn to be able to keep things in perspective. And when he did, not only was he able to enjoy his achievements, even if they weren't perfect, but he was also able to use each one as a building block for holistic happiness.

DOES IT REALLY MATTER?

The American computer scientist Alan Kay once remarked that 'perspective is worth 80 IQ points'. Being able to distinguish between what matters and what doesn't, and being confident to action the former and ignore the latter, is crucial in the pursuit of happiness. Some things you will never achieve (after all, no one can do absolutely everything), but do they really matter? If they don't then there is no point in worrying about them. It is what the philosopher Suzanne Provins termed 'wasting good worrying', and it is a sure-fire way to needlessly impair your ability to be happy. So keeping things in perspective, and learning to determine at the earliest opportunity whether or not they are important to you, and if so, how important, is a vital skill to master. Don't forget that any time spent worrying is time lost to the enemies of happiness, and time spent trying to achieve something that doesn't really need achieving, and which won't add to your life's happiness once it is achieved, is time during which you could have been happy that's simply been thrown away. Instead, discipline yourself to get into the habit of analysing each new problem, opportunity, occasion, etc. and working out whether it is:

- something that is unavoidable
- something that will enhance your life
- worth spending time on

If the answer to either of the first two is 'yes' then the key is to determine just how much time and effort to put into it, and this should be determined by how much reward you are likely to get out of it. And if the answer to the first two points is 'no' then you should simply ignore it and move on, devoting your resources to more productive pursuits.

HOLISTIC HAPPINESS

By keeping things in perspective, you will achieve two important things:

- You will not fall into the trap of wasting time, effort or worry on things that don't warrant it.
- You will ensure that you take a whole-life view, where things are not seen in isolation but are instead seen as individual facets that go to making up your whole life, and your whole potential for happiness.

By taking a holistic approach to your happiness you will be best placed to take full advantage of the opportunities for happiness that present themselves, and to avoid the many pitfalls and pratfalls that can get in the way. Often, when you are too close to a problem, two damaging things occur:

- You cannot see properly what needs to be done in order to remedy the situation, and often take a much more laborious route to doing so.
- You cannot see the scope of the problem, and almost inevitably you will imagine it to be bigger and more damaging than it really is.

By stepping back from the problem, to gain that all-important critical distance, you will be able to see clearly what you are up against, and also how best to deal with it. It is also worth bearing in mind that perspective not only alters how big or small a problem may be, but also whether it is a problem or not in the first place. They say that one man's meat is another man's poison, and something which to one person might be a real headache, might to another be a very small problem, or even something that is beneficial. So remember to look all the way round every potential problem to gain the necessary perspective to enable you to deal with it properly, and to make the most of any potential opportunities it presents.

KEEP THINGS IN PROPORTION

It is all too easy to lose perspective on a problem, and when this happens the usual result is to imagine the worst of each new situation, and its potential for causing unhappiness. This can occur even to people who are naturally optimistic, and is usually worse at night, and when you are tired. It is important to remember not to allow yourself, or circumstances, to blow things out of proportion. Remember that unhappy times are finite, and that the possibilities for happiness are infinite. Try, then, to always remember to look at the big picture, and to remember each thing's worth to you. If it isn't important then there is no point in worrying about it; if it is, then resolve to do something about it straightaway. And always try to keep things in perspective.

Putting it all together

One of the downfalls of not keeping things in perspective is that problems can quickly take on a life of their own. When our perception of a situation is distorted, and the problems appear to be larger than they really are, the natural inclination is to hit the panic button, ready to deal with the large difficulty at hand; and then it is all too common to start to see problems where they don't really exist, and to forget that the problem might not necessarily be a problem at all, since it might not need to affect us.

It is therefore crucial to not allow problems to escalate unnecessarily, either in reality, or just in your mind. When things seem to be more damaging or problematic than they really are, your imagination goes into overdrive and inflates the problem. By remembering always to keep things in perspective you will prevent problems from appearing to be larger than they really are, and by ensuring that you always bear in mind the context in which the problem exists, and the degree to which it is important to you, you will be best placed to keep the situation under control and manageable.

37 You are happy – you just don't know it

> 'Instead of comparing our lot with that of those who are more fortunate than we are, we should compare it with the lot of the great majority of our fellow men. It then appears that we are among the privileged.' Helen Keller

> 'Most folks are as happy as they make up their minds to be.' Abraham Lincoln

> 'Don't wait around for other people to be happy for you. Any happiness you get you've got to make yourself.' Alice Walker

> 'The truth is, belonging starts with self-acceptance. Your level of belonging, in fact, can never be greater than your level of self-acceptance, because believing that you're enough is what gives you the courage to be authentic, vulnerable and imperfect.' Brené Brown

> 'If I had known what it would be like to have it all – I might have been willing to settle for less.' Lily Tomlin

A man once came into a large sum of money, sufficient to buy him all the things of which he had ever dreamed. Straightaway he set about surrounding himself with every luxury and extravagance, and he also made many new friends along the way. For a while he enjoyed his new wealth, but gradually, as the novelty wore off, he began to realize just how unhappy he was. His new 'friends', he had noticed, wanted to see him less and less, and were only interested when he offered to take them all somewhere lavish or exotic, and to foot the bill. His enormous mansion, of which he had been so proud when he first acquired it, now seemed ominously large, and he found that he was living in just a few of its rooms. His supercar had become something of a burden, as he couldn't drive it on public roads the way it had been designed to be driven, and it only garnered jealousy and annoyance from other road users. And so it was, for everything.

Then, one day, the stock into which he had invested almost all of his money lost almost all of its value. He lost the house, the car, his so-called friends and his new lifestyle. Overnight, he found that he was back where he started. But there was one vital difference. This time he was happy. Unburdened by his wealth, he was free to enjoy things again, and he found that he was gaining pleasure from the small things in life, too, of which there are so many. The friends he made were his friends because they liked his company, not because they liked his money. His house was comfortable, and his car was practical and unostentatious. And then it dawned on him – he had, in fact, been happy before he became wealthy, he had just been too busy trying to get rich to notice.

DO YOU HAVE FOOD AND WARMTH?

If the answer to this is 'yes', as it is for the vast majority of people in the developed world, then you are already better off than millions of people; furthermore, if you live in the developed world, you have at your disposal more luxury than the majority of people will ever know – and quite possibly fewer real concerns. After all, if you don't have to worry about where your next meal will come from, or whether you will be able to survive the elements during the next drought, or bout of freezing weather, and so on, or what will happen to you if you fall ill, then you are in a pretty fortunate position really, in the grand scheme of things. This isn't said to sound worthy – rather, that it is simply a fact, and one which it is all too easy to lose sight of in our day-to-day lives.

Of course it is inevitable that you will have problems in your life, some bigger than others, but it is worth always trying to bear in mind how they compare to those of others, not just in your social circle, but on a global scale. Remember that your needs are very different from your wants, and while we all have dreams and aspirations, and most of us have thought through our bucket list of what we would do and buy if we suddenly came into a lot of money, our lists of things we actually need is very different, and very seldom thought through. Happily, if you take a moment to do this you will probably find that you already have everything on your list, or else that it would be a simple matter to get it, and doing so every now and then is a very useful exercise to remind yourself that in the grand scheme of things you are indeed lucky, and happy.

REFRAMING THE PROBLEM

How often do you come across a difficulty, and stress about it, and worry yourself as to how you can overcome it, only for it to resolve itself a short while later with little or no intervention from you? Or else a problem that seemed huge, with potentially far-reaching consequences, turns out to be much smaller than you had feared, and easy to deal with? Often the problem lies not so much in the actual issue at hand, as with our perception of it. And when you start to fear the problem, and its ramifications, the situation can rapidly go downhill. A good way to avoid this is to take a moment to properly assess not only the situation, but its impact on you. Maybe you don't have a large house with a swimming pool and a cinema room — but do you really need these to be happy? Rather, reframe the situation to see it in its true light. It might seem ideal to have these things but if you have all you need, and a bit more besides, then are you not already in a position to be happy?

After all, gratitude is a form of happiness. And just as many lottery winners wish they had never come into money, so it might be with you. Or maybe you feel that you don't have enough hours in the day, and so you never manage to find the time to sit down and do something you really enjoy, such as reading or doing a jigsaw puzzle. But by reframing the problem, and seeing it not as a lack of time but instead a need to prioritize and reorganize your time, you may well find you can free up the time you desire. In other words, you already have what you need, you just need to learn to see it for what it is. So try to look at each situation from a variety of angles, and reframe them to your best advantage.

COMPARISON IS FUTILE

Be careful not to fall into the trap of comparing yourself, and your situation, either to others or to where you feel you ought to be in your life. Try to focus on what you have, not on what you thought you might have had by now, or what you think you ought to have. Look at what you have achieved, not at what you haven't. And you will always know someone who has more, or who has done better than you have, but always remember two things:

- They may seem to have more than you do, but this doesn't necessarily mean that they are happier as a result.
- You may not have as much as they do, but do you need it in order to be happy? Or are you allowing yourself to fall into the trap of feeling inadequate, simply because they have more?

It is worth remembering that sometimes having less is a blessing, and that whatever you have or don't have, you can still be happy. Indeed, many people are truly happy without possessing much of anything, because their desires do not lie in acquiring expensive trappings but in their relationships, their children and so on. So try to identify the positive elements of your situation, whatever they may be – you may be surprised to discover just how happy you really are.

Putting it all together

If you were to take a moment to list all those things that make you happy, or which you feel you would need to have in order to be happy, how many of them would be material and how many would not? And how much of what you don't have can you easily get, or else is something that you don't actually need to make you happy? Perhaps having a Ferrari would be on your list – but do you need to own one in order to be happy, or can you be happy without one? And would such ownership really be as good as you imagine, or would there be headaches and problems that go with it?

Crucially, in what way do you feel that it would make you happy, and can this be achieved in another, more realistic way? It is true that many of us already lead lives that have the potential to make us much happier than we allow them to. The problem is that because we are prone to becoming fixated with what we don't have, what we might have, what other people have, and what we feel we ought to have, we lose sight of what we actually need in order to be happy. And once you learn to see things in that light, it is amazing just how happy you can really be.

Many of us already lead lives that have the potential to make us much happier than we allow them to.

(38) Don't settle for acceptance

❝ *'If you haven't found it yet, keep looking. Don't settle. As with all matters of the heart, you'll know when you find it. And, like any great relationship, it just gets better and better as the years roll on.'* Steve Jobs

❝ *'Once you say you're going to settle for second, that's what happens to you in life.'* John F. Kennedy

❝ *'The minute you settle for less than you deserve, you get even less than you settled for.'* Maureen Dowd

❝ *'The biggest human temptation is to settle for too little.'* Thomas Merton

❝ *'If you are not willing to risk the unusual, you will have to settle for the ordinary.'* Jim Rohn

An intelligent and motivated woman went to university to read law, intending to become a lawyer. She attained a good pass, and as she couldn't get a job practising law straightaway, she got a temporary job as a general assistant in the offices of a large company. She kept applying to firms of solicitors, but then was promoted to the role of office manager. It wasn't a job she particularly enjoyed but she was good at it, and earned a reasonable salary, and took out a mortgage on a house. In due course, a position opened up in a firm of solicitors and she was offered the job. She turned it down, however, because it would initially mean a drop in salary (even though in the medium to long term it would mean a significant increase) and although she could manage financially, she would have to cut back on some of the luxuries she had come to enjoy.

As the years rolled by she became comfortable in her job, although she still yearned to be a solicitor. Every so often she would muster the enthusiasm to apply for a job, but whenever she was offered one she would find an excuse not to take it. Eventually she decided that a good halfway step would be to become an office manager in a firm of solicitors, but this only served to remind her of what she was missing. By now she was in her 30s, and saw people ten years younger than she was doing the job she had so badly wanted. She also saw how much more money they were making, and how much fun they had in their jobs, and in the shared camaraderie. But by now she felt she was too old to start again, to take the initial drop in salary, and to start at the bottom of the ladder, so she decided to settle for what she had. Or rather, she just drifted. She wasn't happy in her job, or her life, but she had settled on accepting her lot. As the years went by, her situation seemed worse and worse as she saw people who graduated after she did earning huge salaries and commanding a great deal of respect in their profession, in jobs that they obviously loved. And as the years went by, she became more and more resentful, and more and more regretful that she had allowed herself to settle for acceptance.

YOU DESERVE TO BE HAPPY

If you are not happy in your life, really and truly happy, then things need to change – because, simply, you deserve to be happy. Everyone does. Yet far too many people just settle for what they have, living life without experiencing all the joys it can bring. This, of course, is different to deserving fame and fortune (which often doesn't bring happiness anyway); it is simply having the right to experience happiness routinely. And nobody can expect to be happy all of the time, but if you are not happy most of the time then it's time to do something about it. This, of course, can be difficult, and often some of the steps that will be required will necessitate hard decisions and awkward choices, but if you believe that the end result will be worth it then do whatever it takes to make it happen.

The American journalist Sydney J. Harris once famously said that: 'Regret for the things we did can be tempered by time; it is regret for the things we did not do that is inconsolable.' And there can be few regrets that are as significant as that of having lived your life unhappily. Often it is those who lack self-esteem who are willing to settle for whatever life gives them, not believing that they have the absolute right to be happy. But, of course, they do because everyone does. So whatever your situation, and whatever your aspirations, remember that you deserve to be happy, and take life by the scruff of the neck to make it happen.

YOU HAVE THE POTENTIAL FOR GREATNESS

The American entrepreneur Bo Bennett once remarked 'Every day, people settle for less than they deserve. They are only partially living or at best living a partial life. Every human being has the potential for greatness.' Exactly what that 'greatness' amounts to will, of course, differ from person to person, but the principle is certainly sound – to achieve your maximum potential for happiness you should strive to reach your full potential in all areas of your life. By doing so, not only will you give yourself the boost that comes from real satisfaction by reaching new goals, but you will also develop new skills along the way that can then be employed to further enhance your happiness in your day-to-day life. So make a list of things you want to achieve in your life, review it to ensure that your goals are realistic, and then go for it – try to achieve as many as you can, starting with those that are most likely to produce the greatest results. Bear in mind that 'greatness' doesn't have to mean doing something notable on a global scale, like becoming a prime minister or winning a Nobel Prize, it just has to be something that equates to greatness in your life. And that is attainable for everyone.

MAP YOUR FUTURE

If you drift through life with no clear vision as to what you want to achieve, and by when, then you are almost certain to achieve mediocrity and to miss out on many wonderful opportunities for happiness. It is only by planning, and then executing, a strategy for happiness that you can make it happen. Not doing so is simply another way of settling for what you have, even if it doesn't make you happy, or even have the potential for doing so, and settling for something that doesn't make you happy is a sure-fire way of ensuring that you won't be.

So plan your future, don't just wait for it to happen to you. If you are truly happy, all of the time, then great. If not, work to ensure you are, by setting your sights on attainable goals, goals which you know will make you happy when completed. You may also be able to engineer the process to be enjoyable, further enhancing your facility for happiness. Crucially, ensure that you avoid the trap of prevaricating and procrastinating, and that you decide quickly on which things you are going to achieve first, and that you then actually get on and do them! In this way, you will also benefit by always having something to look forward to.

Plan your future, don't just wait for it to happen to you.

Putting it all together

If you believe that you deserve to be happy, and if you are not presently as happy as you would like to be, then it's time to do something about it. You have the potential for greatness in your life, so set about mapping your future to be the way you want it to be, and planning what you will need to do in order to make it happen. Settling for what you have, meekly accepting it as your lot rather than challenging it and changing it, is a recipe for unhappiness. Taking the positive steps necessary to turn your life around, in whatever ways are necessary, is empowering and motivating, and will enable you to reach your full potential for happiness.

Settling for, and being accepting of situations that are barriers to your happiness is, clearly, detrimental to your long-term ability to be happy, so this is a situation that must be avoided. However, doing so can be easier said than done. One of the problems is that such situations have a tendency to creep up on you, unnoticed, over time, and you can find yourself entrenched before you have even spotted the danger. Another is that to break the cycle often requires a lot of willpower and hard work, and this can be difficult to implement, particularly when a nagging voice at the back of your mind keeps telling you that things aren't so bad as they are really!

39 'Good enough' is not good enough

❝ *'Perfection is not attainable, but if we chase perfection we can catch excellence.'* Vince Lombardi

❝ *'Aim at perfection in everything, though in most things it is unattainable. However, they who aim at it, and persevere, will come much nearer to it than those whose laziness and despondency make them give it up as unattainable.'*
Lord Chesterfield

❝ *'Success is the result of perfection, hard work, learning from failure, loyalty and persistence.'* Colin Powell

❝ *'A perfection of means, and confusion of aims, seems to be our main problem.'* Albert Einstein

❝ *'Have no fear of perfection – you'll never reach it.'* Salvador Dalí

In the late 19th century an acclaimed engineer set out his philosophy:

'Strive for perfection in everything you do. Take the best that exists and make it better. If it does not exist, invent it. Accept nothing that is "nearly right", or "good enough".'

With this as his mantra, he set out to design and build a motor car, and in partnership with a young pioneer in the emerging fields of motoring and aviation, he did just that. His partner was Charles Rolls, and the engineer was Henry Royce. Their first

Rolls-Royce motor car debuted at the Paris Salon in December 1904, and the Rolls-Royce marque has been the benchmark for quality in the motor industry, and a byword for excellence generally, ever since.

But why is it so important to strive for perfection in everything, all the time? Well, it's not, not for everyone – but it was vital to Henry Royce.

What is important to understand is that this approach to life not only resulted in the creation of fantastic cars, but in happiness for the man creating them. Indeed, on his deathbed, he is said to have uttered: 'I have only one regret – that I did not work harder.' By understanding what it was that made him happy – the feelings of fulfilment gained through hard work, and the success and rewards they brought, he was able to focus on achieving these, in order to bring him happiness.

So if doing everything to a standard that is 'good enough' makes you happy, then that's what you should do – but it rarely is. Rather, there are likely to be certain aspects of your life, those that are less important to you, and where it is not worth doing something every bit as well as it can be done – indeed, this would be a waste of time – and others that are where you will want to focus your resources, particularly your time and energy, to achieve the best possible result, and thereby the maximum possible happiness.

ONLY SWEAT THE BIG STUFF

Henry Royce focused on his work, and achieving as close to perfection in it as he could, because that was what made him happy. In order to achieve similar happiness in your life, you will need to decide what are the elements where it is advantageous to focus your resources, and what can be left at a less perfect level. By prioritizing in this way you will have a much better chance of achieving your goals since you will be spending your time and energy on only a few things, the things that really matter to you.

Remember that these might not be 'projects' as such, such as building the best car or climbing Everest, but they might be areas in your life that you want to get the most out of, such as spending time with your family, or getting really good at tennis, etc. By working out where 'good enough' is good enough you will free yourself up to work on the areas where it isn't.

So if, for example, you realize that you're not spending enough quality time with your children, and that this is an area of your life that needs to change in order to make you really happy, then spend the time necessary to work out how you can make the necessary adjustments in order to free up your time, at the right time – when the children are still awake, but not doing homework! Prioritization and focus are the keys, and following these simple steps can result in improving your level of happiness, quickly and fully:

- Work out which areas of your life you want to focus your attention on.
- Decide what changes you need to make to your life in order to be able to do this.
- Implement the changes.

DON'T CHANGE FOR CHANGE'S SAKE

It's easy to think that by changing an area of your life you can make yourself happier, without really thinking it through. You will need to be aware of the consequences, not only to the areas on which you are going to concentrate but also to the areas on which you are going to spend less time and energy. So don't just implement changes for their own sake, but only if you are clear that:

- The result will be worth it.
- You have the necessary resources to make it happen.
- The other areas of your life that will not have your focus really don't matter as much.

Once you are clear on this, however, it is worth spending the necessary time to ensure that you are clear as to the changes you will need to make in order to be able to focus on the most important ones to you, and that you will be able to see them through.

MAKE IT HAPPEN

Once you've decided what you are going to change, you will need to think through how you are going to make it happen.

Let's take improving your tennis as an example. You think that fulfilling your potential and being as good as you can be will make you really happy – so what needs to change? Do you need to join a club, or switch clubs? Do you need a coach? Do you need to enter tournaments? Do you need to spend more time on your game? And so on.

Make a list of everything that needs to happen, and then work out how you are going to achieve each one, e.g. What adjustments do you need to make in order to free up enough time to take lessons? Do you need to earn more money, or spend less money elsewhere, to make these possible. And, crucially, once you've worked out exactly what you need to do, you need to actually do it! It's amazing how often well-intentioned plans never come to fruition not because they weren't workable but simply because they weren't seen through.

A good way to help to ensure that yours are is to make a timeline for achieving them, and then regularly monitor your progress, making adjustments where necessary.

Putting it all together

When things are nearly right they are actually wrong, at least in part. And while it's not possible to achieve perfection in every area of your life, by deciding which parts you want to make your focus, you will be able to concentrate your efforts where they matter most.

By enabling yourself to achieve the best possible results in these key areas you will give yourself every opportunity to improve your level of happiness in a meaningful, and sustainable, way.

So in the things that really matter to you, don't allow yourself to settle for anything less than the best. Remember that in

these key areas 'good enough' really isn't good enough –
push yourself to achieve the very best you can, then allow
yourself the time to enjoy the results. You will need to be
ruthless when deciding which things to change, and which
not to, since your resources are finite, and if you spread
yourself too thin you are only setting yourself up to fail,
which is both pointless and demoralizing.

You will also need to be clear about which areas of change
are realistic and which are not, since reaching for unattainable
goals is equally damaging to your happiness. So take the time
to get it right, choosing the areas that are both important to
you and which really can be changed, and where the change
really will make you happier, and then go for it!

40 You don't want to be rich

" 'He is richest who is content with the least, for content is the wealth of nature.' Socrates

" 'Desire of having is the sin of covetousness.' William Shakespeare

" 'In a country well governed, poverty is something to be ashamed of. In a country badly governed, wealth is something to be ashamed of.' Confucius

" 'It is health that is real wealth and not pieces of gold and silver.' Mohandas K. Gandhi

" 'Be careful to leave your sons well instructed rather than rich, for the hopes of the instructed are better than the wealth of the ignorant.' Epictetus

After many years of soul-searching, a successful millionaire realized that he was unhappy, despite his lifestyle. Indeed, he came to the conclusion that he was unhappy because of it. Despite having just about everything that one could possibly want, or else having the means by which to acquire it, he felt unfulfilled and so, with a wholeheartedness that was typical of the man, he set about changing things. And what he did was something that most people would find very difficult to even imagine doing.

He simply gave away his entire fortune.

He decided that if he even kept sufficient to enable himself to live in comfort for the rest of his life it wouldn't be enough, and so he set about finding places and institutions to which he could give away all his money. Then he moved into very modest accommodation, and realized that he was experiencing something quite special. It was as if a terrible weight had been lifted from his shoulders.

THE POSITIVES OF POVERTY

Someone once said that money can't buy you love, but it can certainly strengthen your bargaining position! The truth, of course, is that money can indeed open doors to opportunities for happiness – but it can also cause great heartache and misery, a fact shown by the many lottery winners who say they wish they'd never won.

One of the problems with setting your sights on earning (or winning!) a lot of money is that it is all but impossible to know when you have enough. To put it another way, if you already have enough money to buy food to eat, and to put a roof over your head, keep you warm, etc. – in other words, to provide all the necessities – then you have everything you actually need and so anything extra is surplus. So since we have established that this is money you don't need, with how much surplus will you be satisfied? If you don't have a definite end point then how can you possibly know when to stop? And if you do have an end point in mind, the chances are that its position will shift as you earn more money, so that you end up needing to earn more and more and more money just to keep up.

If you originally thought that you would be satisfied when you could afford a nice house and a fancy car, will you really be able to stop when you have them? Or will you instead start looking enviously at your neighbours' even bigger house, or even fancier car, and want to earn enough money to get something similar? And when you have those, what about something bigger and fancier still? And so on.

There really is no end to it, and so unless the pursuit of money makes you happy, rather than actually earning it and spending it, then it is very unlikely that this model will be satisfying to you – and thus unlikely to bring you happiness.

On the other hand, someone with much less, but who is satisfied with what they have, may well be happier. So constantly striving for more money is unlikely to make you happy, but a realization of how lucky you are to have what you do have probably will.

THE TWO TYPES OF WEALTH

There are two distinct, and in many ways opposite, types of wealth: there is the wealth of having a lot of money, and with it a lot of material possessions, and there is the wealth of being truly happy. And interestingly, the only real reason for people wanting to acquire and retain the first is so that they can experience the second.

So it is true to say that it is the second of these, attaining happiness, which is the goal – acquiring money is simply a means to an end to help to achieve this. So what happens if it doesn't? What happens if instead the wealth that is so painstakingly gained serves only to undermine happiness, or even to destroy it?

In this case, surely it is far better not to have it in the first place. So why are so many of us striving to attain more and more wealth?

As with so many things, it is the degree to which it is taken that is so often the deciding factor. Money gained, in moderation, may well make you happy, since it will allow you to own and to experience nice things, without becoming a victim of your success by becoming burdened by it. If you don't know when to stop, however, this can all too easily become the case.

So how do you know when to cease the quest for ever more money? Quite simply, when you have achieved your aim – not simply to make more money (for which there might never be an end point), but to be happy. For this reason, it is imperative that you monitor your position frequently and do not allow yourself to become lured by the promise of more, more and more, but instead to always remember why it is that you want money, and why it is that that will be damaged by the over-accumulation of it.

HEALTH WEALTH

It is true that a healthy poor man will often be happier than a wealthy ill one. In the same way, finding peace in your life, learning to fully relax (and giving yourself the opportunity to do so), and making sure that you are content is far more important than busting a gut to try to earn more and more money. It is not that there is anything inherently wrong with money, or the accumulation of it – it is that all too often we lose sight of why it is important to us and allow it to govern our lives to the detriment of everything else.

If making money is all that you need to do in order to be happy then that's fine – but for most people it isn't. So try to find moments of calm in your everyday life, and remove yourself from the stressful rat race so that you can focus on what matters to you, on what really makes you happy.

The world can be a hectic place, full of noise – both literal and metaphoric – and finding time every day to enjoy some peace and quiet, to relax, and to focus on feelings of happiness and wellbeing may well be more valuable to you than any amount of money.

Putting it all together

Money can be both a blessing and a curse, and often at the same time. Not enough of it can lead to stress, worry and unhappiness. Too much of it can do exactly the same. By understanding the role of money in your life, and how it can make you happy (without blithely assuming that it's just a case of the more of it you have the happier you'll be), you will be able to determine how much of it you need, and how much of your life, of your time and energy, you want to devote to its pursuit.

If you cannot think why you want to earn, or win, the money you desire, then it is likely that money is controlling you, and not the other way around. If your goal is to be happy, not simply to make money for the sake of it, then you need to determine how much you need to make this happen, and what sacrifices you are willing to make so that it does. Just remember that real and lasting happiness is your true objective, and that money is only useful to you as far as it helps you to achieve this.

41 Richly poor

 'Less is more.' Ludwig Mies van der Rohe

 'He is now rising from affluence to poverty.' Mark Twain

 'Focusing your life solely on making a buck shows a certain poverty of ambition. It asks too little of yourself. Because it's only when you hitch your wagon to something larger than yourself that you realize your true potential.' Barack Obama

 'You can turn painful situations around through laughter. If you can find humour in anything, even poverty, you can survive it.' Bill Cosby

 'As you simplify your life, the laws of the universe will be simpler; solitude will not be solitude, poverty will not be poverty, nor weakness weakness.' Henry David Thoreau

When the technology firm Apple, having lost its way and struggling in the computer marketplace, rehired Steve Jobs, he realized at once that one of its major problems was that it was simply trying to be successful in too many areas, all at once. Despite employing great people, they were stretched too thinly to be able to focus on getting anything through to completion quickly, and brilliantly. And so he culled the number of projects – from several hundred, to just four. It was a daring, bold and courageous decision, but very quickly it proved to be a masterstroke. The company was producing just a few things, but each of them was a 'must-have' item for millions of people, and as a result the company soon boasted a turnover amounting to billions of dollars, with its brand becoming one of the most important in the world.

Jobs had realized that the answer was not to try to make everything they were capable of making, but rather to choose just the most important few designs and make them better than anyone had imagined they could be made. And by concentrating on so few projects, it ensured that the company was able to put behind each one the requisite money and people to make it successful. It has been said that less is more, and with its innovative approach, Apple had neatly proved the point. By focusing on fewer projects, the company was able to do more with each of them, and by doing so didn't need to decide between having either quality or quantity, but was instead able to produce quality, in quantity.

So it is with happiness. If you try to change every aspect of your life to improve your happiness, the chances are that you will be inundated with possibilities and that you will end up not being able to complete any of them (as well as being overwhelmed by the workload, which in itself is likely to make you unhappy!). Rather than try to do so much, and only doing each to a cursory degree, it is far better to concentrate on just a few and see them through to completion. In this way, you will be able to achieve a quality result with those you opt to undertake, so the key is to ensure that you select the right ones.

And once these are finished, why not select just a few more to take their place, always ensuring that you don't take on too much, and that you see each through before moving on.

QUALITY NOT QUANTITY

The key is to choose just a few projects, and to make sure that you are able to finish them before moving on. Since you will only be selecting a few projects it is worth taking your time to ensure that the ones you select really are those that will provide you with the most return for your effort; you will also need to ensure that they are sustainable in the long term.

Try to choose projects that will not only improve your happiness to the maximum degree, but ones that will also enhance your happiness in as many areas of your life as possible. Remember that you are only going to take on a few, so make sure that you choose wisely.

One of the pitfalls of this approach, and it's one into which people often stray without even realizing it until it's too late, is that as you get a project underway, other opportunities or difficulties arise as a result. If you're not careful these can quickly escalate to become fully-fledged subprojects, and even grow into full-scale projects in their own right. Without careful, and ruthless, management, you can easily find that before you know it your carefully selected three or four projects have spiralled into many, many more, and your chances of completing each successfully and punctually have diminished by the same degree.

You will therefore need to be always on your guard to ensure that you stay focused and on-project. Indeed, you might even find that after a careful and thorough audit of your life as it stands, you really only need to change one key area in order to make a real difference to your happiness, allowing you to focus completely on this, and making it easier to ensure you don't become sidetracked.

SIMPLIFY YOUR LIFE

We have more opportunities today to do things, experience things, have things and manage things than at any time in history, and the temptation to fill your life with as many as you can is often overwhelming, since we are constantly bombarded with them, from all directions.

There is also a fear of missing out, fuelled by hearing about everyone else and what they are doing, and how well they are doing, which drives us to feel that we have to let more and more into our lives. But the truth is that things will only be beneficial to us, and bring us happiness, if they are meaningful to us, so select carefully those things in which you want to invest your time and energy, and don't fill your life with meaningless clutter. Be careful not to throw the baby out with the bath water though — hold on to what makes you happy, and improve upon it.

LEARN TO FOCUS

How many times have you begun something that you will enjoy, and then become sidetracked by other things that demand your attention, and either never returned to your original project, or else found that you have not been able to continue with it in the same way, and with the same enthusiasm? Someone who enjoys building model aeroplanes was telling me that every time he sat down to enjoy his hobby, something would inevitably happen to interfere with his plans and disrupt his model-making, so that in the end he couldn't be bothered to get out all the necessary materials and set himself up to begin since he knew that there was a high likelihood that interruptions would scupper his plans.

When he analysed what was causing the interruptions, he found that the majority were caused by either the telephone ringing or else someone in his household requiring his attention. Rather than just give up on something that was bringing him joy, the solution was simply to become unavailable to everyone, unless there was an emergency.

It took a little while, and some perseverance, to establish a workable routine, including letting his friends know of his plans so that they wouldn't take offence if he didn't come to the phone when they called, and ensuring that his wife and children knew when he was going to work on his model, and that they always had sufficient warning that they could speak to him first if they needed to. He also decided with his family that he would only do this twice per week, and never for more than two hours at a time, but by working out a way to fit it into his life, and make it work for everyone, he was able to continue enjoying a hobby that brought him much joy and satisfaction. He also decided to watch less television at the weekends, and to cut out the various ways he managed to waste time with fruitless activities, and to make sure that he spent some quality time with his family.

So by reducing the number of things he did, and focusing on the one that mattered the most, he was able to ensure he found time to properly enjoy it.

Putting it all together

Sometimes loading yourself with myriad possibilities for happiness only serves to obscure those possibilities that are also practical, achievable and useful. Having the opportunity for happiness is not enough, you need to act on it – and that's a lot easier to do if you concentrate on a manageable number. Prioritization is the key, so list all the options open to you, and then plot them on a simple graph with those that are easiest to implement at the far left of the x-axis versus those that are most problematic or time consuming on the far right. Then, on the y-axis, plot those things that you feel will bring you the most benefit, right at the top, versus those whose improvement to your life will be more marginal, at the bottom. Now divide the graph into four equal squares by drawing a line straight down the middle, and another across the centre. Now discard everything except the top left corner. The items here will be those that are easiest to implement, and which will provide the most benefit. Lastly, select a maximum of four, and get started.

42 The wealth of poverty

> 'He that is of the opinion money will do everything may well be suspected of doing everything for money.' Benjamin Franklin

> 'Money won't create success, the freedom to make it will.' Nelson Mandela

> 'After a certain point, money is meaningless. It ceases to be the goal. The game is what counts.' Aristotle Onassis

> 'I thank fate for having made me born poor. Poverty taught me the true value of the gifts useful to life.' Anatole France

> 'Many people take no care of their money till they come nearly to the end of it, and others do just the same with their time.' Johann Wolfgang von Goethe

Imagine two people, both perfectly content in their lives, and both of whom win a fortune in a lottery. One decides that all his life's worries are at an end, and celebrates his good fortune by buying a large house, a fast car and booking expensive holidays. The other opts to tell no one of her windfall and to give it all to charity. Over time, the first person gets used to his new life, and as the novelty wears off he realizes that since this is now his routine, it is no more exciting than his old life was. Also, without having adequately invested a portion of the money, it gradually dwindles until he is forced to sell off his possessions, and finds himself back where he started. Now, however, he is no longer content with his life as it is, since he has experienced something 'better', something he knows he will almost certainly never see again, and every time he sees a wealthy person he is filled with resentment, jealousy and greed.

The second person, meanwhile, never experiences such a dramatic change in her lifestyle, but as she was content to begin with she doesn't mind. Each time she remembers her lottery win, however, she is filled with an inner peace and sense of happiness and satisfaction, knowing all the good her money did; and each time she sees someone in poverty, either in real life or else in the media, she is reminded of her philanthropy and is deeply happy. And as the years go by, this feeling never wanes – in fact it grows, as the sense of pleasure deepens in the knowledge of all those people whose lives have been improved as a result of her actions. And her life, meanwhile, does not suffer any detrimental changes, but continues as before, in perfect contentment.

'Poverty' is, of course, a relative term, and so is 'wealth', but it is not always those who have the most money who are happiest, and it is not always money that is the measure of positive possessions.

WHAT IS WEALTH?

This might seem like a question with a very obvious answer, and indeed most people would judge their wealth, and that of other people, by how much money they have. But perhaps a better criteria is to first determine what it is that makes us happy, and then to see how much of it we have. If money is the only thing on your list, then that indeed is all you need to focus on. But it is far more likely that your list will comprise a host of elements, each of which are important to you in their own right, and which all together provide the platform that provides you with the greatest happiness.

Common entries on such a list include time spent with family members, time spent on enjoying a hobby, listening to music or watching television, going for walks in the countryside, giving to charity, helping other people, going on holiday, sunny days and balmy evenings, and so on. Your list can be as long or as short as you want it to be, but try to include all those things that have a significant impact on your happiness. Then determine how much of them you already have – and you might be surprised at just how wealthy you already are. By looking at ways to improve your lot by means of the items on your list, such as finding more time to enjoy reading a good book, or making the most of good weather when it arrives, you can increase your wealth significantly, without too much effort. So by redefining 'wealth', not simply as money and possessions but as the richness of our lives, it is perfectly possible to makes ourselves wealthier any time we want to – and that has to be worth doing.

WHAT IS POVERTY?

In the same way, we can redefine 'poverty' so that it doesn't simply mean how much or how little money we have, but how rich or poor our lives are in terms of how much we enjoy living them. If someone is perfectly happy with very little, then they cannot really be said to be poor, even if they have little in the way of money or possessions. Real poverty, then, can be defined as when our lives are structured in such a way as to not allow us to be happy. If we live from day to day without regularly experiencing happiness, in any of its many forms, then not only are we living in 'happiness poverty', but we are doing so unnecessarily. Many of the things on your list are likely to be freely available – all that is required is an adjustment to your lifestyle to enable you to enjoy them. So make your list, then make the necessary changes to the way you live your life, and escape poverty into a newly enriched life.

MONEY, MONEY, MONEY

We have looked at alternative definitions of 'wealth' and 'poverty' from those we would normally associate with these terms, but let's take a moment to look directly at the issue of money, since it is an inescapable part of modern life. For one thing, without at least a certain amount of money we can't put a roof over our heads, or buy enough to eat, and these fundamentals must of course be taken care of if we are to be happy. A lack of money can easily lead us into 'happiness poverty', too, since it is all too easy to borrow money, and to borrow more than we can really afford, leading to mounting debt – one of today's prime factors in causing depression and worry. But money alone will not make you happy – so how can we turn material wealth into 'happiness wealth'?

Money can help to bring you happiness or it can have the effect of doing just the opposite. Often the key is to know your limits and to take things one step at a time. Too much, too soon, can easily lead to disaster, as the great many lottery winners who say they wish they'd never won will confirm. Also, it is important to know what you want the money for. This might sound obvious, but it really isn't. How would you spend it, in a way that would enhance your life, and without verging on the danger of your wealth spoiling things for you? What do you need, in order to be happier, that only money can bring? And how much do you need? By having a clearer understanding of these things we can be confident of using money in the most appropriate way to bring us, and others, happiness; and it may well become apparent, too, that we don't require nearly as much money as we thought we did to create in our lives the maximum potential for happiness.

Putting it all together

Wealth and poverty both have relevancies to happiness outside of the context of money. 'Happiness wealth' and 'happiness poverty' are more complex, and in many ways more important than simply how rich or poor you are in material terms, since the financially poorest people can be the happiest, and the financially wealthiest may be the least happy. Money can be useful in that it can help to bring you happiness in a variety of ways, but only if it is employed wisely – it is rarely the object of the exercise in itself. By redefining what we mean by 'wealth' and 'poverty', and by rethinking our relationship to money, we can access new routes to happiness, more quickly, and even discover new types of happiness to enjoy.

Thinking of your happiness in terms of wealth and poverty can also be useful since it takes it beyond simply thinking about how much or how little of it you have, and instead puts the focus on quality just as much as quantity. Thus the degree of your happiness becomes just as important as how often you are happy, and this is absolutely relevant since it can be more beneficial to be truly joyous once per day for a brief spell, than to be reasonably happy for twice as long. Seeking to maximize your happiness may need a complete rethink of your approach, as well as the fundamental aspect of what happiness means to you.

43 Buy your way to happiness

> ❝ 'Money has never made man happy, nor will it, there is nothing in its nature to produce happiness. The more of it one has the more one wants.' Benjamin Franklin

> ❝ 'All I ask is the chance to prove that money can't make me happy.' Spike Milligan

> ❝ 'Money can't buy happiness, but it can make you awfully comfortable while you're being miserable.' Clare Boothe Luce

> ❝ 'It's a kind of spiritual snobbery that makes people think they can be happy without money.' Albert Camus

> ❝ 'Desire nothing, give up all desires and be happy.' Swami Sivananda

Two prizes were offered to winners in a national 'Lotto' game – they could choose between receiving a lump sum of US$1 million, or to receive US$2,000 each month for the rest of their lives. Most of the lucky winners opted to have the lump sum, keen to head off on a shopping spree straightaway, and thrilled at the idea of becoming an instant millionaire. They bought large houses, fancy cars, yachts and second homes. Unfortunately, many of them failed to think through the long-term cost of living in their newly elevated lifestyle, and soon they were having to sell off some of their possessions, at a loss, in order to keep the others. The heartache they experienced was sufficient for some off them to attempt to sue the game's organizers for having failed to warn them of the danger.

For the minority who chose to have the regular payments, though, the story was quite different. Since their money was drip-fed to them they weren't ever in a position to dramatically change their lifestyle overnight, but instead they were able to 'upgrade' it over time. In this way the process was more organic, and more sustainable, and their expenses were only ever as much as they could actually afford. One man who opted for this prize surprised the game's operators since he was in his early seventies at the time of winning. They explained to him that he would have to live in excess of another 40 years before he would have received the same amount of money as he would if he took the lump sum, and that although they hoped he would, the odds were against it. He, however, was unperturbed, knowing that such a windfall was more likely to make him miserable than it was to make him happy, while the US$2,000 each month he could enjoy spending for the rest of his life.

HOW MUCH MONEY WOULD YOU LIKE?

Can money really make you happy? And is the love of it really the root of all evil? Money, misused, can certainly bring you grief. So too can an all-pervading desire for more of it, no matter how much you already have. But money is not, in itself, a bad thing; nor is it, however, a good thing – it is how it is employed, what its real worth is to you and what it can bring you that count. In trying to become as happy as possible, it is important to understand the role of money in your life. What is its role now? And what would you like it to be? Just how big a part of your life is it, and how big would you like it to be? And how important is it in your life, and how important do you feel it should be? It is certainly an inescapable part of modern life, but is it a necessary evil or something to be enjoyed and celebrated? The answer lies in your relationship with money, and whether it is something that causes you more worry than joy, or vice versa. Interestingly, a sufficiency of money usually brings harmony, while both a lack and a surplus have the capacity to bring discord.

HOW MUCH IS TOO MUCH?

Most people tend to think that they would love to have lots of money, and that although it might bring its own problems, they would be nice problems to have! We have already seen, however, that too much money can cause terrible problems, but a little extra for luxuries often brings happiness. If you already have sufficient disposable income to enjoy then all well and good, but if you don't then you will need to ascertain the following:

- How much would you ideally want?
- How important is it to you?
- What are you willing to do, or to sacrifice, to get it?

The first point should be considered with a nod towards reality, not dreamland, and should be decided with a view to remembering that too much money can bring real problems. So how much would actually make you happy? Once you have decided this, you will need to find your answer to the second point, in order to determine what your answer to point three is. You might decide that you want to reallocate some of your money, either by spending your disposalable income in a different way, or else by making more of it disposable; you might decide that you are prepared to do more work in order to make more money, and that the sacrifice in time and effort will be worth the reward; or you might elect to cut out something for which you currently pay, in order to spend the money in other ways. Whatever you decide, make sure that you always have as your guiding principle the goal of making your money work harder at making you happy.

MONEY ISN'T EVERYTHING

It has been said that the most valuable thing you can give is your time, and the most precious commodity that can be spent is other people's time. Money certainly isn't everything, and it should always be remembered when finances dwindle that you probably have a lot else for which to be grateful – which of course is a form of happiness. Are you fit and healthy? Do you have a roof over your head? Do you have enough to eat today? And so on. So even if your disposable income has been disposed of, you still have plenty of reasons to be happy. And if a lack of money is causing you anxiety then don't allow the situation to persist – grab the bull by the horns and sort it out, whatever that takes, such as downsizing your home, or being ultra-strict with your weekly shop, etc. And just as a lack of money isn't everything, nor is a surplus of money, so always be careful to assess your situation to ensure that your financial situation is causing you to be happy, not stressed.

Putting it all together

Money can't buy you happiness, but it can certainly strengthen your ability to be happy. This only holds true, however, provided you are clear as to what you want your money to enable you to do, and why you want to do it. Money for money's sake is useless – money as a tool for improving your happiness is valuable indeed. Remember to use all your assets – money, talents, contacts, skills, etc. – to promote happiness in your life, and always prioritize being happy. At the end of the day, being happy in your life allows you to live your life better, and if you are happy then those around you are also likely to be happy.

44 Everyday miracles

 'Miracles happen every day, change your perception of what a miracle is and you'll see them all around you.' Jon Bon Jovi

 'Miracles do not, in fact, break the laws of nature.' C. S. Lewis

 'Miracles come in moments. Be ready and willing.' Dr Wayne Dyer

 'A strong positive mental attitude will create more miracles than any wonder drug.' Patricia Neal

 'Love is the great miracle cure. Loving ourselves works miracles in our lives.' Louise L. Hay

Annie was a very bright girl, who matured into an intelligent and conscientious woman, and it came as no surprise to those who knew her when she was accepted into Oxford University. She opted to read law, and when she graduated with a first-class degree she had her pick of law firms, all vying to gain her services. She settled on one of the most famous and most prestigious in London and quickly cemented her reputation as one of the best young legal minds in the country. She had it all – money, position, respect and a great future mapped out for her. Except for one thing – she was unhappy. Although she now had everything she had aspired to and worked so hard for, she found that she wasn't happy. Something was missing, some element that would make it all right.

One day, as she travelled to work on the Underground, she sat opposite a woman with a tiny baby, no older than a few weeks, and she soon fell into conversation with her. Afterwards, Annie couldn't remember what they had talked about, but she knew she would never forget the look on the woman's face, a look of pure joy. Even though the woman was clearly exhausted from the relentless demands of looking after her baby, it simply didn't seem to matter to her, and in that moment Annie knew what she had to do. To the surprise of all her colleagues she handed in her notice, and returned to university, this time enrolled on a completely different course. Three years later she graduated as a fully qualified midwife, and began working in a busy central London hospital. She was used to working long hours in a demanding job, and this was certainly no different, and just as highly pressurized, but this time she was happy in her work since every day she got to witness a miracle, the miracle of birth, and often more than once. She knew it was something of which she would never tire, and every single time she held a newborn baby, and saw the look on its mother's face, she felt elated, exhilarated and purely happy.

STAY ALERT

Everyday miracles, on every level, occur all around us all the time, but often in a hectic world they go unnoticed. Not only is this a pity for the people concerned, it is a wasted opportunity for everyone else too, because by taking advantage of noticing and enjoying these mini miracles you can benefit from the joy they bring. It could be as simple as an unseasonably warm, sunny day in winter, or the birth of a baby, or someone we know experiencing sudden good fortune, but whatever it is it can serve to lift our spirits, often unexpectedly. Often all it takes is a change of attitude, and an increased awareness of what is happening around us. By remaining ever alert to the wonders apparent in so many situations, every day, and by adopting the right mindset to notice them when they occur, you will begin to see them often, and sometimes in the most unexpected of places or occasions, and each has the potential to be uplifting and inspiring. Learn, also, to see good things in unexpected people and places, and develop the skills and mindset to enjoy them.

OTHER PEOPLE'S SUCCESS IS YOUR SUCCESS

You will naturally be aware of, and enjoy, your own successes, but if you can become accustomed to enjoying other people's successes, too, you will immediately substantially increase your opportunities to experience happiness, and at no cost, and very little effort, to you. It is greatly rewarding to enjoy other people's achievements, successes and happiness, and often these occur in areas that are not those where they would usually occur in your own life, so they add an element of surprise and discovery which in itself can be uplifting and rewarding. By learning to enjoy the successes of others, you will be provided with many more opportunities to experience a soul-warming 'feel good' moment than if you only enjoyed your own achievements and triumphs.

Of course, the wider you cast your net, the greater will be the opportunities presented to you, so try to include as many people and situations as possible. These need not be limited to people you are in regular contact with, or even just to people you know, but can include friends of friends, famous people, sports teams, and so on. It has never been easier to follow the careers and fortunes of others than it is today thanks to the uptake of social media, so if you enjoy Facebook, Twitter, LinkedIn and the like, you will be able to gain inspiration and satisfaction from a wide variety of sources quickly and easily, and delivered directly to you in the comfort of your own home. Happiness really doesn't get much easier to experience than that!

LOVE YOURSELF

Alan Cohen once said: 'To love yourself right now, just as you are, is to give yourself heaven. Don't wait until you die. If you wait, you die now. If you love, you live now.' It is true that unless you are happy about yourself, it is difficult to be happy about just about anything else. Most people would say that there is room for improvement in their life, and that's fine, but if you don't deep down, in your heart of hearts, when no one else is looking, love yourself then your whole view of life will be coloured with that negativity. How you feel about yourself underpins everything that you feel about other people, and informs every experience you have, so loving yourself is crucially important.

That doesn't mean that it is necessary to think that you are perfect, since imperfect people can be perfectly loveable (thank goodness!); it means that you must have a deep-rooted belief in yourself, and your worth, as an individual, and utterly believe that you are a good person with lots of great qualities. It shouldn't matter what you look like, what you do for a living, how wealthy, influential, powerful, etc. you are or are not – all that matters is that you love yourself for what you are. Remember to tell yourself this every now and then, and make sure that you mean it. Find time for yourself every day, and look in the mirror and like what you see. List some of your best qualities, write yourself a love letter – whatever works for you. Just remember that unless you love yourself, not only is it difficult for you to love others, and for them to love you, but your ability to be happy on any level will be severely impaired.

Putting it all together

Miracles, whatever you perceive them to be, happen all around us all the time, if only we would notice them. If you can't think of the last time that you noticed one – indeed, if you can't remember right now several that you've seen recently – then it's time to reevaluate what you think of as a miracle, and to learn to be ever-conscious of the opportunities to witness them, every day. By training ourselves to be on the lookout for life's wonders, however small they may be in the grand scheme of things, we can open ourselves up to a host of possibilities for enchantment and happiness, in things that are just there without any effort on our part, and which would otherwise go unnoticed. Indeed, it is this ability to see what's there for what it is, and not just taking things for granted, that can exponentially increase the chances of being happy on a continual basis.

One of the most common barriers to adopting this sort of attitude is the lack of self-love, self-worth and self-belief, which affects so many people. In today's world of hearing about so many wonderfully successful people all the time, and seeing so many glamorous and beautiful people every day courtesy of the media, it is little wonder that our opinions of ourselves often take a battering. Just try to bear in mind that often you only hear half the story, and that plenty of the images you see have been digitally manipulated. Forget about other people, do away with comparing yourself to anyone else, and just love yourself, and your life, for what they are.

45 The mania of calm

66 *'The language of excitement is at best picturesque merely. You must be calm before you can utter oracles.'* Henry David Thoreau

66 *'Remain calm, serene, always in command of yourself. You will then find out how easy it is to get along.'* Paramahansa Yogananda

66 *'Never be in a hurry; do everything quietly and in a calm spirit. Do not lose your inner peace for anything whatsoever, even if your whole world seems upset.'* St Francis de Sales

66 *'When adversity strikes, that's when you have to be the most calm. Take a step back, stay strong, stay grounded and press on.'* LL Cool J

66 *'I have so much chaos in my life, it's become normal. You become used to it. You have to just relax, calm down, take a deep breath and try to see how you can make things work rather than complain about how they're wrong.'* Tom Welling

In the centre of a large and thriving city, where life is lived at a hundred miles an hour, and where hectic is just a way of life for many of its busy residents, lies a surprising oasis of calm. It occupies only a modest area, and on every side the world rushes by, but within its walls there is a peace and tranquillity of which most people can only dream. The building is unprepossessing and probably goes unnoticed by the majority of people who pass its facade, and inside it is no different, kept deliberately unfussy and uncluttered, with only the minimum of apparel and a noticeable lack of luxuries, technology, or the majority of the myriad trappings of modern living most people take for granted. But while the decor might be stark, and the furnishings meagre, the residents would tell you that they want for nothing, for this is a monastery, where poverty and simplicity are a way of life, and where the days are spent in prayer, reflection and quiet meditation. The days are structured, and while they are long, they are unhurried, and there is plenty of time built in for leisure too. The pervading sense is of calm, and peace – and a quiet, contented happiness.

Of course, the monastic life certainly wouldn't suit everyone, or indeed perhaps most people, but bringing a little of the monks' tranquillity into our everyday lives would certainly be beneficial. In particular, the spread of modern technology can easily mean that we fill every waking moment with some sort of stimulus, never giving ourselves pause – that necessary space in our day to quietly reflect, and be at peace with ourselves.

We have already seen that there are many different types of happiness, but that which is provided by serenity is perhaps one of the easiest to overlook, and one of the simplest to implement.

WELCOME POSITIVE STRESS AND BANISH NEGATIVE STRESS

Stress is a part and parcel of everyday life, and often inescapable, so how can you make sure that it doesn't impinge negatively on your life, and get in the way of you being happy?

First, it is important to understand that there are two types of stress – positive and negative. When we think of stress it is usually of the latter type, and the way that it impacts detrimentally on our life, but the former type of stress forms an important part of the arsenal we need in order to function at our best – without which we have much less of a chance of being happy.

Positive stress, such as that experienced before giving a speech, or taking an exam, can give us a vital edge, heightening our senses and our wits, and providing an important spur to our energy, and to our ability to perform to our maximum ability.

This type of stress should not, therefore, be avoided but should be welcomed, and even engineered for those moments when it will serve us well. Just be careful not to stay in this heightened state for too long, nor too often, since it can be tiring and will take its toll if overused.

The other sort of stress is negative stress, and this is almost always damaging to our ability to be happy. This type of stress comes in a variety of forms, including anxiety, worry, depression, long-term difficulties, extreme and prolonged nervousness, etc. Since its impact is nearly always detrimental to our ability to be happy, it needs to be avoided whenever it is possible, and combated quickly when it is not. In order to avoid as much negative stress as possible, it is important to understand where and when in your life it is most likely to occur, and the ways in which it is most likely to manifest itself. In this way, you will give yourself the best chance of avoiding the situations that cause it, and thus circumventing the stress itself. If it simply cannot be avoided, it will need to be dealt with, and this, too, is easier if you have seen it coming and prepared for it.

By minimizing its impact on your life, although you will not have avoided the negative stress, you will have avoided most of its ability to cause you grief, in turn maximizing your ability to remain happy.

YOUR BEST SHORT CUTS TO PEACE AND TRANQUILLITY

Try thinking of the times when you have best experienced peace and tranquillity, and the chances are that they will have occurred at times in your life when you have been the most receptive to calm. Interestingly, they may also have occurred in very similar places.

It is almost impossible for us to feel peaceful and serene when we are fraught, anxious, over-tired, etc., so it makes sense that in order to experience deep and lasting peace we first need to ensure that we give ourselves the best possible chance, and this usually means removing ourselves from the many disturbances that could otherwise shatter it.

Try taking yourself out of your normal environment, perhaps by going for a long walk somewhere tranquil, and make sure that your mobile phone is switched off. Make sure that you have enough time to be able to enjoy the serenity, and then spend the first part of your allotted time thinking through all those things that could interrupt your peace, and get them squared away in your head.

Then just allow yourself to be in the moment, enjoying whatever is around you right there and then, and focus on the calm of it.

You will soon find yourself experiencing a deep peace, and if possible make sure that you have enough time to enjoy it afterwards, too, so that its effects can linger, doing you the most good, for the longest time.

EVERYDAY, ANYWHERE, TRY A SPOT OF INSTANT MEDITATION

Whenever you have a spare moment and want to step out of the rush of the day and into a pool of instant tranquillity, try this simple exercise.

First, find a quiet space – it doesn't matter where, but try to make sure that it is somewhere where there is unlikely to be anyone interrupting you. Close your eyes, take a deep breath, and clench all your muscles. Then, slowly, relax your body while exhaling. Next, think of the place you last went to when carrying out the previous exercise, and focus on one particular part, perhaps a wood, or a meadow. Try to remember as many details as you can: what the weather was like; whether it was warm or cold; what it smelled like; whether there were other people around, and so on. Try to remember how you felt when you were there, how peaceful it was, and how uplifted and released from tension you were. Enjoy the sensations again, while breathing slowly in and out, and letting your muscles all loosen. Finally, when you are ready, breathe in deeply while slowly opening your eyes, and enjoy the sense of peace your instant meditation has given you.

Putting it all together

Stress, and the sheer busyness of our everyday lives, can quickly lead to unhappiness if you are not on your mettle to combat them. By always keeping a weather eye open for situations and occasions that can cause such unhappiness you can move to quickly remedy them, either by minimizing their impact, or else by avoiding them altogether.

You can also aid your cause by becoming adept at determining quickly which stresses in your life are positive and which are negative, so as to maximize the former while minimizing the latter. You can also work to lower the impact of negative stress by carrying out exercises designed to imbue peace and tranquillity in your life, and by mentally 'saving for a rainy day' such times so that they are there to be called on whenever necessary.

46 Focus your focus

'I find hope in the darkest of days, and focus in the brightest. I do not judge the universe.' Dalai Lama

'That's been one of my mantras — focus and simplicity. Simple can be harder than complex: you have to work hard to get your thinking clean to make it simple. But it's worth it in the end because once you get there, you can move mountains.' Steve Jobs

'Most people have no idea of the giant capacity we can immediately command when we focus all of our resources on mastering a single area of our lives.' Tony Robbins

'Focus on the journey, not the destination. Joy is found not in finishing an activity but in doing it.' Greg Anderson

'Goals provide the energy source that powers our lives. One of the best ways we can get the most from the energy we have is to focus it. That is what goals can do for us; concentrate our energy.' Denis Waitley

When an engineer had reason to use a wheelbarrow, and discovered a number of flaws in the basic design, he set about creating something better. Instead of a wheel, which was prone to sinking into soft ground, and lacked stability, he decided to use a ball, and the 'Ballbarrow' was born. Next, he turned his attention to the vacuum cleaner. Frustrated with the inefficiency of the standard model at the time, whereby power was lost every time the bag became full, he set about creating a completely different type of cleaner. It still used a vacuum, but the bag was gone – and so was the loss of suction.

But if that sounds easy, consider this – it required a total of 5,127 prototypes, over a period of 15 years, before the model was perfected to his satisfaction. What is truly remarkable is that nowhere along the line, while making the 5,126 vacuum cleaners that did not work or match up to his standards as he would have wished, did he give up; nor did he dilute his focus by turning to other areas in which his research, and new designs, might be employed. By concentrating his focus in just one area, and working continually to perfect the device, he revolutionized vacuum cleaners forever.

Once his creation became successful, he moved on to hand-dryers, bladeless fans and heaters, each time working to perfect the new creation before moving on. The engineer was, of course, James Dyson, and today the British technology company, Dyson Ltd, sells machines in more than 50 countries and employs more than 4,000 people worldwide.

SPREAD YOURSELF FAT

In seeking to gain the maximum possible happiness in our lives, it is imperative that we focus our energy and our abilities on the most productive way to make this happen.

In order to do this, you will need to first identify those areas in which you think an improvement will produce the greatest and most tangible benefits to your happiness, and preferably in the shortest possible time and with the minimum of effort, so that you know where to concentrate your efforts, at least initially.

Spreading yourself too thin and trying to change, all in one go, every facet of your life to bring you more happiness, is a recipe for achieving very little in a great many areas. What you want to do, instead, is to achieve a lot in just a few key areas. In this way, you will derive the maximum benefit in the shortest possible time, because those things that you decide to make your focus will be done properly, and will start to yield meaningful results, whereas lots of things only half done will yield significantly poorer results.

In order to ensure that your life is improving in those areas you had anticipated that it would, you will need to monitor the situation and be prepared to make continual adjustments as necessary. This, too, will be easier if you have a strong, clear focus. So decide where your priorities lie in order to gain the maximum additional happiness in the shortest time and with the least additional effort, then focus your resources just in these areas.

THE POWER OF ONE

It stands to reason that if focusing your time, effort and energy on improving just a few areas of your life that you have identified as key to enhancing your happiness, then by concentrating all your resources on just one area you will achieve the maximum possible focus – and with it, the maximum reward.

Think through all the areas of your life in which you believe you can improve your happiness, and look to see if one stands out above all the others. If it does, either because you think that it will yield the most benefit, or because you have identified an area that will yield an important benefit and will do so quickly and easily, then focus all your effort in this one area, and this one area alone, to see the power of focusing your resources at work. Not only will the improvements in this area come about quickly, they will also be easier to see and to monitor, as they will be unobscured by other improvements. And once this one area has been tackled, which should happen relatively speedily anyway since it's where you are devoting all your resources, you can move on to the next most important area, and so on.

Another benefit to this approach is that if the improvement to your happiness will only come about once the area has been fully tackled, then by doing just one and moving on, you will feel the benefits much more quickly than if you elect to tackle several projects, the results of which will take several times as long to be seen.

TOTAL AWARENESS

Knowing what you want to achieve, and how you're going to achieve it, and devoting yourself completely to attaining that one end, is crucial in order to secure the best possible chance of reaching your goals, and in the minimum possible time, and with the minimum expenditure of resources. At the same time, however, you must be careful to avoid becoming too insular and inward looking, for fear of missing opportunities for happiness 'quick wins' that might present themselves at any moment.

Imagine someone who has identified that their priority is to find more time to enjoy their passion, gardening. They have also highlighted their desire to get the upstairs windows cleaned, to take up tennis and to buy a new car. They concentrate their focus brilliantly, but do so at the expense of being able to benefit from other opportunities that may present themselves unexpectedly. By maintaining a perspective on the bigger picture you can ensure that you do not miss any golden opportunities to quickly and easily improve your happiness, while at the same time ensuring that you never split your focus and risk diluting your energies – and your results.

Putting it all together

A focused, targeted approach is the most direct route to achieving your goals. Whatever it is you set out to achieve, by concentrating your efforts in just a few key areas – or, if possible, on one single area – you will reach your goals in the shortest possible time, and with the fewest resources. In this way you will begin to benefit more quickly from the lifestyle changes you have implemented than would be possible if you were trying to implement a number of changes all at once, making you happier, faster.

Imagine trying to implement ten changes all at once, and devoting one tenth of your resources to each, and that at the end of ten months they are all completed. From this point onwards you will be happier in ten different ways, but for the duration of those ten months you will not have benefited in any way. Instead, focusing on one change and seeing it all the way through to its conclusion means that you will begin to benefit from that change after just one month; then you can begin to implement the second change and so on. In this way you will have completed all your changes in the same period of time, but you will have benefited from them as you go along, adding one more each month. Furthermore, it is likely that you will have achieved each goal in less than one month, since you will not have spread your focus. So if you can complete each change in half the time by focusing on just one change at a time, you will have completed the entire transition in five months instead of ten, as well as having benefited from each change as you go along, adding a new one every two weeks.

47 By yourself, you're never alone

❝ *'If isolation tempers the strong, it is the stumbling-block of the uncertain.'* Paul Cézanne

❝ *'Isolation is the sum total of wretchedness to a man.'*
Thomas Carlyle

❝ *'Our language has wisely sensed the two sides of being alone. It has created the word loneliness to express the pain of being alone. And it has created the word solitude to express the glory of being alone.'* Paul Tillich

❝ *'Yet it is in this loneliness that the deepest activities begin. It is here that you discover act without motion, labour that is profound repose, vision in obscurity, and, beyond all desire, a fulfilment whose limits extend to infinity.'* Thomas Merton

❝ *'There is no way that writers can be tamed and rendered civilized or even cured. The only solution known to science is to provide the patient with an isolation room, where he can endure the acute stages in private and where food can be poked in to him with a stick.'* Robert A. Heinlein

Violet was one of the most vibrant people you could ever hope to meet, the life and soul of any party, and with no shortage of friends. Yet, she was lonely. Recently retired, she missed the everyday camaraderie of the office, the daily banter, and although she had been looking forward to retirement since she would no longer have to face the dreaded hour-long commute, she had

9
10
11
12
13
14
15
16
17
18
19
20
21
22
23
24
25
26
27
28
29
30
31
32
33
34
35
36
37
38
39
40
41
42
43
44
45
46
47
48
49
50

223

also known that she would miss her colleagues, and the regular contact with other people her job provided. But she hadn't known how much. And to make matters worse, nobody else knew of her predicament, since she always seemed so cheerful, but she was only cheerful because she was with other people, and as soon as she was alone again she felt desperately lonely. Worse still, she didn't like to admit to feeling lonely, and so told no one of her plight.

Then one day, while she was out for a walk (which she did not so much for the exercise as to see other people and perhaps engage some of them in a brief conversation), she noticed a sign advertising free computer lessons at the library. Her job hadn't required her to use a computer, and she had never had much interest in them, so she had never learned, but now she saw an opportunity to spend time with other people on a regular basis, and she jumped at the chance. Every Wednesday she would spend a convivial hour learning about computers, and soon she saw the possibilities for communication and connectivity that they afforded, and she was hooked. She bought one of her own, and quickly became a regular contributor to numerous online forums, and soon discovered a host of information on a wide variety of topics that were of interest to her. She had found for herself a new lease of life, and made some new friends, and resolved to join a number of other groups so that she had some real-world contact every day.

ISOLATION AND LONELINESS

There is a reason why prisoners whose wills their captors are determined to break are kept in isolation. The lack of human connection, and the inability to communicate and interact with others, can be extremely damaging to the spirit. In seeking to maximize our happiness, it stands to reason that we need to minimize our unhappiness. In order to do this we need to minimize the occasions when we expose ourselves to situations that might be injurious to our wellbeing – and one of the main culprits in this area is loneliness.

It is important to remember that loneliness is not necessarily the same thing as being alone. There are plenty of people who live in busy metropolitan areas, and may even have contact with people on a regular basis, who are nevertheless consummately lonely since they do not experience the intimate connection that comes from interacting with friends, family and loved ones. Equally, there are people who enjoy being alone, and who do not find that such isolation causes them to feel lonely. For the majority of people, however, being alone for a significant length of time causes loneliness, so unless isolation is self-imposed because it is desired, it is something to be avoided. Fortunately, in today's super-connected world, there are more opportunities to avoid loneliness than ever before.

We can invite people into our homes virtually, through television, radio, the Internet, etc. or we can communicate with people remotely, either by telephone or, increasingly, via communications that allow us not only to speak to the other person but to see them as well, such as FaceTime and Skype. We can cherry-pick our communities, to get involved with other people who share our interests by joining groups online, or by following those which interest us on Facebook, Twitter and so on. We can communicate with people easily and instantly, and sometimes the challenge is knowing where to stop! The other side of the coin, however, is that although we can be connected all the time it can still feel lonely if it is not person-to-person at least some of the time, so try to ensure that you build a network of people with whom you can spend time on a regular basis, and that you have regular, real-life contact with people whose company you enjoy.

KEEP YOURSELF CONNECTED

If we have more opportunities than ever before to keep ourselves connected by utilizing modern technology, but that this means alone is insufficient, then we need to find ways of keeping ourselves connected in the real world. By finding the right opportunities, not only can we avoid the unhappiness associated with isolation, but we can also take advantage of new opportunities for enjoyment, and therefore happiness. One of the easiest ways to do this is to join a club or society that revolves around one of your hobbies or interests — and if you don't have one, this is the perfect opportunity to discover something new. A hobby can be rewarding and fulfilling, both of which are direct routes to happiness, as well as allowing us to meet other people – people who share our interests, and therefore with whom we have something in common. By joining a group, attending classes or belonging to a society, you will also have the opportunity to improve in your chosen field, and this ability to learn new skills or to improve existing talents is a great way to boost your happiness while at the same time circumventing a possible means of unhappiness.

ALL BY MYSELF

Staying connected is all well and good provided it is possible, but what happens when it is not? If there is nobody with whom you can communicate on a regular basis, either person-to-person or virtually, then you will need to adopt a different approach in order to safeguard your happiness. This means learning to experience real happiness on your own, and is a skill that can take time to perfect, but it is certainly possible to achieve if you approach it in the right way. First, you will need a positive mental attitude; you have decided to take this route, or else it has been forced on you, but either way you must be determined to enjoy the opportunity and to make the most of it. For a start, you must not think of it as isolation, but solitude, and not as something to be endured but as something to be savoured. But with this approach, too, you will need to develop your interests. Common pursuits include reading, jigsaw puzzles, photography, and watching television and listening to the radio, but whatever your preferred means of engagement you must be sure not to let the fact that you are by yourself prevent you from engaging in some way.

Putting it all together

Isolation and loneliness, unless deliberately chosen, are to be avoided at all costs, since they are two of the most common reasons for unhappiness. Communication and connectivity are key, and where possible this means engaging with other people, either virtually or in the real world. By identifying areas of interest you have in common with others you can find new means of enjoying shared experiences, as well as enjoying the boost that comes from improving your skills.

Where possible, at least a portion of your communication and connectivity with others should be in the real world, but virtual means of achieving this end should not be overlooked, since they can add significantly to the amount of time you spend avoiding isolation, and they can be extremely valuable as a supplement to real-world interaction. If there are times when it is not possible to interact with others – either in the real world, or virtually by means of modern communication and connectivity outlets – then you will need to find ways of enjoying the enforced solitude. This is perfectly possible provided that you put in place a positive action plan to avoid any potential loneliness, and that you ensure that such periods are limited, with a predefined end-point whenever possible.

48 Don't get boxed in

> 'A year or so ago I went through all the people in my life and asked myself: does this person inspire me, genuinely love me and support me unconditionally? I wanted nothing but positive influences in my life.' Mena Suvari

> 'And I have to work so hard at talking positively to myself. If I don't, it's just real hard to get through the day, and I'll get really down, and just want to cry. My whole body language changes. I get more slumped over.' Delta Burke

> 'A positive attitude causes a chain reaction of positive thoughts, events and outcomes. It is a catalyst and it sparks extraordinary results.' Wade Boggs

> 'Some people never contribute anything positive to society, they may even drain our resources, but most of us try to do something better, to give back.' Martin Yan

> 'I think it's important to get your surroundings as well as yourself into a positive state – meaning surround yourself with positive people, not the kind who are negative and jealous of everything you do.' Heidi Klum

Soldiers who are possibly in danger of capture in war are trained in techniques that will help them to resist interrogation, and even torture. During drills they are kept in isolation and mistreated in any number of ways, including being deprived of food and sleep, as they are put through a regime designed to weaken them, both physically and mentally, and to break their resolve to resist. One of the key techniques they are taught is how to remain positive, no matter how dire the situation may seem. One way this can be accomplished is to analyse every situation and to identify and draw on three positive things from it. This can, of course, be extremely difficult in a situation such as that described, but it can always be done. The list of positives in this example, may, for instance, include such things as:

- still being alive
- labelling your captors with unflattering names
- frustrating your captors by not giving in, so that you are winning – and they are losing.

Amazingly, by taking this approach, soldiers are often able to deal not only with the situation at the time, but also afterwards, when they manage to suffer virtually no ill-effects as a result of their experiences. This may be an extreme example of one technique of keeping positive in any situation, but it serves to highlight just how powerful such techniques, properly used, can be. And if they work in such extreme conditions, then they can certainly work in the sort of everyday situations most of us are likely to face where we feel we need a boost.

This is an extreme example of one technique of keeping positive in any situation, but it serves to highlight just how powerful such techniques, properly used, can be. And if they work in such extreme conditions, then they can certainly work in the sort of everyday situations most of us are likely to face where we feel we need a boost. Importantly, strategies like this for keeping yourself cheerful, even against the odds, require no one but yourself to make them work, and nothing but willpower to put them into practice.

ATTACKING ANXIETY

Anxiety, in any form, is a dangerous barrier to happiness. Not only does it cause worry and distress, but it also forms a tangible barrier to being able to experience happiness of any sort. A passive approach, simply hoping the anxiety will go away and waiting for it to pass, is unlikely to satisfactorily resolve any issues. Such a negative approach is more likely, in fact, to have the opposite effect, allowing the anxiety to take hold and even to grow. The best way to deal with the anxiety, therefore, is to attack it. A positive approach, where the sufferer refuses to be the victim but instead takes control and deals with the anxiety head on is much more likely to yield positive results, and to do so more quickly.

A useful technique in dealing with anxiety is one that follows the old adage that 'prevention is better than cure'. This involves thinking through your life, both your day-to-day routine and on a wider basis, and identifying those occasions when you are likely to be prone to suffering some sort of anxiety. You will then need to develop a strategy for dealing with these situations, either by avoiding them in the first place (the best strategy where possible) or else by learning how to negate their impact, and move past them quickly. By taking this proactive approach, and not waiting until you are anxious before trying to deal with the issues, you will be tackling them not when you have been laid low by worry and stress, but when you are at your strongest.

AVOIDING DISTRESS

Learning how to shield yourself from anxiety is a great start, but in order to secure a positive environment, one in which you can be truly happy, you will need to go further than this. Another common form of distress, which acts as a barrier to happiness and is often present in day-to-day life, is that of negative imaginings. These often occur at night, or when you are on your own, and can take many forms including worrying (about your finances, those you love, your career or a forthcoming interview, etc.), and fear (about the future, your situation, dangers (both real or imaginary)) and often strike when you're at a low ebb, compounding the problem.

Again, the strategy for dealing with them, and thereby preserving your ability to be happy, is to identify where and when they are likely to occur, and have in place a mechanism for dealing with them. This might be something as simple as positive thinking (blocking negative thoughts, and promoting positivity), or it might be something more involved, such as having a safe place in your home where you can go when you want to feel comforted, and a routine you like to follow to distract yourself from your negative thoughts, but whatever it is it's fine as long as it works for you, and allows you to avoid unnecessary distress and to feel happy.

DEALING WITH NEGATIVITY

Negativity, of any sort, is an enemy of happiness, since it is impossible to maximize your happiness if you are beset by an underlying feeling of negativity, while positivity is just the opposite. All the time you're feeling positive – about yourself, your surroundings, your job, your home life, your future, etc. – you will have a spring in your step, and you will be receptive to any positive energy coming your way, allowing you to be as happy as possible. So dealing with negativity is crucial in the quest for sustained and meaningful happiness. The first step is to understand what it is in your life that causes you negativity. Try making a list of all the things that you feel are not a positive influence on your life, and all those things that are definitely negative. Then work out which things it is possible to avoid so as not to be influenced by their negativity. For those things that it is not possible to avoid, you will need to have an action plan in place to enable you to deal with them swiftly and firmly; and by knowing what they are, and when they are likely to occur, you will be forewarned and therefore forearmed.

Putting it all together

Avoiding stressful, anxiety-provoking situations is the first step to combating the negativity that they will otherwise surely provide, and knowing what these situations are, and when they are likely to occur, gives you a vital head-start. Sometimes, however, it is simply not possible to avoid these situations, and in these cases it is important to have established in advance what you will do to combat the negative feelings. A persistent positive mental attitude will be a great help, since it will put you in the right frame of mind from the outset, but your defence against unhappiness-causing negativity will need to go much further.

Putting in place a robust action plan will help you to deal with negative situations as quickly and as positively as possible, allowing you to move on at the earliest opportunity. Try to find three positives in every situation, no matter how bad it seems, and try to avoid aggression and negativity both in yourself and others. By avoiding stressful and distressing situations, and by attacking anxiety whenever it occurs, and before it can really take hold, you will maximize your opportunities for mental positivity, a vital bedrock for happiness.

49 Living for now

❝ *'Learn to enjoy every minute of your life. Be happy now. Don't wait for something outside of yourself to make you happy in the future. Think how really precious is the time you have to spend, whether it's at work or with your family. Every minute should be enjoyed and savoured.'* Earl Nightingale

❝ *'Learn from the past, set vivid, detailed goals for the future, and live in the only moment of time over which you have any control: now.'* Denis Waitley

❝ *'Change your life today. Don't gamble on the future, act now, without delay.'* Simone de Beauvoir

❝ *'I wasted time, and now doth time waste me.'* William Shakespeare

❝ *'A good plan violently executed now is better than a perfect plan executed next week.'* George S. Patton

At the age of 22, Gary was enjoying life to the full. He had achieved his ambition of becoming a soldier, a job which he loved and at which he excelled, and he had quickly risen to the rank of corporal. He loved the outdoor life, the camaraderie he shared with the other soldiers in his outfit, and the pride that came from being part of an elite unit, and as a natural sportsman he had been selected to represent both his regiment and the Army at rugby and boxing. He was also engaged to be married, and was living life at a 100 miles per hour, packing in as much as he could every day.

Then came the war. Gary's unit was mobilized, and soon he was fighting a vicious and bloody conflict miles from home. He was unperturbed by this, since it came with the job and this was what he had been trained to do, but he was completely unprepared for the cold February dawn that was to change his life forever. Advancing on an enemy position, Gary trod on an improvised explosive device (IED). He was immediately airlifted to a field hospital, where he underwent emergency surgery, and although this undoubtedly saved his life there was nothing that could be done to save his legs. They had been shattered and torn apart by the force of the explosion, and two months later Gary found himself out of the Army and struggling to come to terms with his new prosthetic limbs. Then, one day, while trying to attach them, Gary found himself ruing what had happened, and what might have been, and was shocked to discover that for the first time in his life he was feeling sorry for himself.

He knew he was at a crossroads in his life, and that the decisions he made now would affect not only what he was able to do, but who he would be, in the future. And so Gary dived onto the Internet, picked up the phone, attended a series of meetings and interviews, and just six weeks after reaching the crucial turning-point in his life Gary arrived at the sports institute for elite disabled athletes. He was trialled for a variety of sports, and found his niche in the game of wheelchair rugby. Gary had chosen to be happy, despite everything that had happened to him, and as a direct result, he was. Two years after losing both his legs, Gary represented his country at the Paralympic Games, and today, in addition to his athletic endeavours, Gary works as a motivational speaker, a great example of just what can be achieved by anyone who decides to live life to the maximum, every single moment.

PLANNING FOR HAPPINESS

In William Shakespeare's *Twelfth Night*, the much-teased and fun-despising puritanical, Malvolio, utters the famous line: 'Some are born great, some achieve greatness, and some have greatness thrust upon them.' It is a sentiment that still rings true more than four centuries later, and could just as aptly be applied to happiness; some people seem to be naturally predisposed to being happy most of the time, while others have to work at it, and some people seem to be happy despite themselves! Whatever your personality and natural predilection, however, by planning for happiness you will maximize your chances of achieving it.

Try thinking through your day in advance and highlighting those occasions that you think you will enjoy, and why. Then analyse them to see if there is any way that you can make them even better, with just a little planning. For instance, perhaps you will be playing tennis this evening, but by rearranging your workload you can leave work 20 minutes earlier, giving you time to purchase some new tennis balls for your game; or maybe you're going out to a restaurant for dinner, and by pre-booking a taxi you will be able to enjoy a drink with your meal. By thinking through your day in this way you may also find some occasions that can be made enjoyable with a little forethought, where otherwise they would simply be beige moments; and you may even be able to turn some occasions that you are not looking forward to into enjoyable experiences. You will also have the added advantage of gaining happiness from the anticipation of enjoyable events.

So by putting in a little upfront effort, and planning and preparing for good times, you can often make them even better.

HAPPINESS REFLECTIONS

As we have seen, it is often possible to make the most of the positive occasions with which we are presented by planning for them in advance. However, it is also important that you enjoy your achievements as well as your plans. This is crucial not only in order to gain the most enjoyment from each occasion, but because it is by maximizing such moments that you can build up a repository of satisfying and heartwarming memories to look back on. Try to get into the habit of taking a mental snapshot during each enjoyable occasion. All too often enjoyable occasions are over before you know it, and taking a moment to step aside and really notice what is going on will help to ensure that it does not simply run its course without being fully appreciated. It will also give you something great to look back on. At the end of every day, try looking back on your day and identifying five key moments when you were really happy. Then mentally store these away so that you can enjoy reflecting on them in the future.

TEMPORARY HAPPINESS VERSUS PERMANENT HAPPINESS

Temporary happiness is easy to achieve. Unless the situation you find yourself in is extremely dire it will nearly always be possible to enjoy fleeting moments of happiness. But in the quest to maximize your happiness, such transient fulfilment is inadequate. What is required is the creation of a situation where the happiness is permanent. This is not to say that you will never experience moments of unhappiness, or that for the whole of your life you will feel euphoric. What it does mean, however, is that you can build for yourself a sufficiently robust platform of happiness that is sufficient to enable you to weather the storms of discontent and unhappiness which will, from time to time, beset you. In this way you will be able to experience temporary happiness even within the framework of an ongoing stressful situation, and a complete and enduring happiness overall.

Putting it all together

By positively and deliberately preparing yourself for happiness you will maximize your chances of achieving it. For many people, happiness is something that is stumbled upon, and which either occurs for them or doesn't without any intervention on their part. Indeed, the very idea of preparing for happiness may seem to them to be rather odd. However, happiness is just like anything else we want to achieve in life. By anticipating it, and preparing for it, we can maximize the chances of it actually happening. Thinking through our day, week, month and even year ahead, and mentally highlighting those occasions that we think will make us happy, we can best ensure not only that they do so, but also that they make us as happy as they possibly can. This approach has the additional benefit of the enjoyment gained through positive anticipation, while at the same time minimizing the chances of the happiness being bypassed, and also allowing us to prepare for moments of negativity, and minimizing them through robust planning. Enjoyable moments should be remembered and reflected upon frequently, both in order to gain further happiness from their memory, and also to inspire us to create future occasions for happiness. Remember that happiness can be both temporary and permanent, and in the quest for maximizing your happiness potential it is important to create a framework in which happiness becomes the underlying and permanent bedrock.

(50) Spying on yourself

> ❝ 'Could a government dare to set out with happiness as its goal? Now that there are accepted scientific proofs, it would be easy to audit the progress of national happiness annually, just as we monitor money and GDP.' Polly Toynbee

> ❝ 'Don't measure yourself by what you have accomplished, but by what you should have accomplished with your ability.' John Wooden

> ❝ 'The ultimate measure of a man is not where he stands in moments of comfort and convenience, but where he stands at times of challenge and controversy.' Martin Luther King, Jr

> ❝ 'I tell people to monitor their self-pity. Self-pity is very unattractive.' Patty Duke

> ❝ 'I don't measure a man's success by how high he climbs but how high he bounces when he hits bottom.' George S. Patton

A factory owner once decided to measure his factory's output. He put in place a number of systems whereby everything coming into and going out of the factory was recorded, as well as expenses incurred, what stock was available and when, and how much profit was being made. Over time, in order to increase profits, he ordered that the prices of the factory's products be increased, and that the materials they were buying in should be sourced for less money, which inevitably meant purchasing inferior materials. He also ordered that a number of jobs be cut in order to increase profitability, and that the remaining workforce should work longer hours, for no extra pay.

Initially the factory's profits soared, and the owner was extremely pleased with himself. He ordered that output be further increased, and extra materials brought in to cope with the increased demand. Then he sat back smugly as he awaited further success. As he continued to measure the factory's output, however, he was alarmed to see that sales were falling. He also noticed that the factory's output was diminishing. Distressed, he set out to discover the reason why. His customers, it transpired, who had always been satisfied with his company's work, were now alarmed by the fall in the standard of the products the factory made, particularly as this had been coupled with an increase in prices, and one by one they were going elsewhere to buy what they needed. At the same time, the once loyal workforce had become disillusioned, and although they were working longer hours, they were doing so with less energy and so the overall levels of output per person had not increased; and since the workforce was now smaller the output had inevitably dropped. Furthermore, the numbers of days being lost to members of staff being off sick had risen sharply. And the stark reality was that the business was in worse shape than ever.

Too late, the factory owner realized his mistake. In his desire to increase his business's profitability he had set out a number of measurement criteria, but he had been measuring the wrong things. He had measured costs, but had forgotten to take into account customer satisfaction. He had measured prices, but disregarded his customers' goodwill. He had measured the output of the workforce, but he had not thought to keep an eye on their morale. Before long the factory was running at a loss, and the owner had no choice but to shut it down.

Measurement is key to determining the success, or otherwise, of any venture, and the quest for achieving maximum happiness is no different, but in order for it to be useful it is imperative to ensure that you are measuring the right things, and that you are not overlooking anything important.

MADE-TO-MEASURE

It is important to keep tabs on your happiness so that you can see if you are letting yourself slip in any area, allowing yourself, even inadvertently, to become unhappy; and also so that you can ensure that you are maximizing your happiness in every area, and all of the time. And if things are not as they should be, then what needs to change? By keeping a constant eye on your happiness you can ensure that you have in place the right systems to maximize it, and that if this is not working in any area, then you give yourself the best chance of noticing it at the earliest opportunity, allowing you to do something about it quickly. So, first things first – what is it that needs to be measured? In order to produce the most useful measurement framework it is imperative that you identify precisely what does, and equally importantly what does not, need to be measured. Create for yourself a checklist of things you wish to keep an eye on, such as the amount of time you are spending on pursuits you enjoy versus the amount of time that is being devoted to things you do not enjoy, or the frequency with which you are experiencing moments of real delight as opposed to gentler forms of happiness. Then, crucially, make sure that you refer to it often, and that if anything isn't working as well as it should be, that you put it right at the earliest opportunity.

METRIC OR IMPERIAL?

So, you've decided what you are going to measure – now you need to decide how you are going to measure it. The easiest and most effective way is to do so on a daily basis. It is very difficult if you leave it until the end of the week (or even the end of the month!) to remember exactly how your days went, how often you were happy or unhappy, and the degrees to which the emotions were experienced, as well as the reasons why. By measuring your happiness every day you will be able to see quickly and easily where things are going well, and where you need to make adjustments. You will also give yourself the advantage of being able to nip in the bud anything that isn't working for you, allowing you to take positive action to remedy the situation. Don't forget that such daily reviews do not need to take long, and will certainly become quicker over time, so that before long you are undertaking them without even really noticing it – they will simply become part and parcel of your everyday routine.

TAKING ACTION

Once you've decided what you are going to measure and how you are going to measure it, you will need to ensure that you have decided how you will act on it. There is simply no point in measuring your happiness if you do not use the information this provides to further enhance your situation, and to put a halt to anything that is proving to be detrimental to your happiness. So make sure that when you review your happiness, you take the time to highlight the areas that are letting you down, and to do something about them. You will need to identify precisely what it is that is not working for you, and then determine the best approach to remedy the situation. If it is possible to implement this immediately then do so, but if it is not then you will need to be clear about the reasons why, and to know when you will be able to get things underway. Make sure that this is a definite point in the calendar, just as you would with any other action that needs to be taken, and that you do not allow it simply to drift. Happiness can be a useful and important measure for your life, and the benefits of rigorous measurement and implementation of action points can be far-reaching and long-lasting.

Putting it all together

Monitoring your situation to ensure you are maintaining a framework and approach that allows you to be as happy as possible for as much of the time as possible is vital in enabling you to take charge of your happiness. You will need to determine which elements of your life are key in allowing you to be happy, and how precisely you will measure their efficacy. You will then need to determine how you are going to rectify anything that is not working, and to maximize the potential of everything that is. By measuring your situation daily, you will enable yourself to keep a firm grip on your happiness, and to ensure that you never allow a day to go by without either gaining from it the maximum happiness that you can, or else identifying the reasons why this didn't happen, and ensuring that the situation will be different next time. In this way you should be able to increase your happiness every day, and as time goes by you should find yourself needing to implement changes less and less.

Discover the secrets behind greatness